Learning
Together

Learning Together

A Manual for Multiage Grouping

Nancy Bacharach
Robin Christine Hasslen
Jill Anderson

CORWIN PRESS, INC.
A Sage Publications Company
Thousand Oaks, California

For information address:

Corwin Press, Inc.
A Sage Publications Company
2455 Teller Road
Thousand Oaks, California 91320

SAGE Publications Ltd.
6 Bonhill Street
London EC2A 4PU
United Kingdom

SAGE Publications India Pvt. Ltd.
M-32 Market
Greater Kailash I
New Delhi 110 048 India

Printed in the United States of America

Library of Congress Cataloging-in-Publication Data

Bacharach, Nancy.
    Learning together: a manual for multiage grouping / Nancy
Bacharach, Robin Christine Hasslen, Jill Anderson
        p. cm.
    Includes bibliographical references and index.
    ISBN 0-8039-6266-5 (C : alk. paper). — ISBN 0-8039-6267-3 (P : alk. paper)
    1. Ability grouping in education.   I. Hasslen, Robin Christine.
II. Anderson, Jill, 1953-   .   III. Title.
LB3061.B33   1995   95-13624
371.2'5—dc20

This book is printed on acid-free paper.

95 96 97 98 99 10 9 8 7 6 5 4 3 2 1

Corwin Project Editor: Susan McElroy

Contents

Preface

Schools in the United States today segregate students by age into grade levels and curricula that presume specific abilities, skills, and interests. The assumption upon which such grouping exists is that same-age children acquire similar knowledge in the same way at the same time. Teachers in these classrooms often believe their role is to impart a prescribed body of knowledge to students on a predetermined timeline. There has been less attention to *how* we teach than to *what* we teach.

The recent and growing focus on developmentally appropriate curricula and practices has led some schools to examine alternative strategies, curricula, and structures. One of the emerging structures is multiage grouping: the purposeful grouping of children who are more than one year apart in age. Within these settings, teachers can provide a wide range of activities to meet a diversity of abilities and interests and can accept a variety of performance competencies as valid.

The transition from traditional classroom grouping to a multiage grouping, however, takes more than a decision to combine children of various ages into one room. The adoption of a multiage model requires a new set of attitudes, skills, and understanding of how children learn. The purpose of this book is to provide (a) an examination of the theoretical basis for multiage grouping, (b) a realistic picture of what it looks like, (c) some guidelines for planning and implementing a multiage model, and (d) recommendations from practicing multiage teachers.

The book is intended primarily for teachers in education at the preschool and elementary levels, for administrators, for parents, and for teacher educators. The field of education is constantly striving for excellence in its practices and programs. It is essential that all people involved in the education of tomorrow's citizenry regularly evaluate the results of their practices. This book will assist educators in that evaluative process as they consider the implications of multiage grouping.

Teachers, administrators, and parents presently examining the rationale behind and/or means to implement the alternative structure of multiage grouping will find this book an extremely helpful guide. Teachers already working in a multiage setting will find support and affirmation for their work, as well as curricula and pedagogical suggestions. Administrators will be provided with the underlying principles of multiage grouping, and thus be better equipped to educate parents and other staff as well. Teacher educators will also find the book helpful in preparing future teachers for varied school structures and diverse student populations.

The first chapter of the book defines multiage grouping and provides a brief history of the movement. Each chapter begins with a case study presenting a perspective of multiage grouping from various players, including students, teachers, administrators, and parents. Chapter 2 supplies the theoretical framework by examining which theories contribute to the creation of a solid foundation upon which multiage grouping is built. Chapter 2 also presents the current research base on social and cognitive effects of multiage grouping.

Chapter 3 provides the readers with the common beliefs and the curricular, instructional, and assessment elements inherent in multiage settings. Although there are no set models for such groupings, there are important elements in which teachers should be grounded, such as process writing, literature-based reading, math manipulatives, thematic teaching, computer-assisted instruction, and the use of learning centers and cooperative learning.

Chapter 4 presents pictures of four sites that are currently utilizing multiage models. The chapter describes each school's departure from a graded structure and some glimpses of day-to-day workings in a multiage setting. Chapter 5 follows with some down-to-earth advice on how to get started and how to be assured that your program will be solid enough to overcome some of the barriers that are inherent in any change. The final chapter pulls all the pieces together by providing teachers' perceptions of advantages and disadvantages, as well as advice and encouragement.

We would like to acknowledge all the teachers who provided input into this book. We have been moved by their commitment to multiage grouping, and even more so by their commitment to their students. In particular we are deeply grateful to those teachers who shared their journeys with us: Roger Anderson, Sue Roepke, Cindy DeWitt, Scott Peterson, Chris Grote, Diane Howe, Joanne Hoveland, Sharon Truex, Shawn Gombos, Linda Cooper, Joyce Cheeley, Edwina Harder, Ruth Johnson, Sandy Dahlager, Kristen Bechtold, Kari Dombrovski, Judy Rotto, Joe Telfair, Sue Foster; and principals, Art Dorman, Mike Trewick, and Chuck Niles.

About the Authors

Nancy Bacharach is currrently an associate professor in the Department of Teacher Development at St. Cloud State University in St. Cloud, MN. She began her teaching career in Wisconsin and taught at the elementary level for 5 years. She received her B.S. from the University of Wisconsin-Eau Claire in Elememtary Education, and her M.Ed. and Ph.D. in Curriculum and Instruction from Texas A & M University. She taught for 3 years in the Division for the Study of Teaching at Syracuse University prior to coming to St. Cloud.

Her major teaching responsibilities focus in the area of reading education, including reading and language arts methods, reading research, and children's literature. She does frequent in-services on multiage grouping and is the organizer of an informal support network for multiage teachers. In addition, she is the co-director of an experimental Inclusive Teacher Education Project that is preparing teachers to work effectively to meet the diversity of children in our nation's classrooms. Her research interests include multiage grouping, inclusive education, multicultural children's literature, instructional practices in teaching reading, and teachers as researchers.

Robin Christine Hasslen received her B.A. in Sociology from Wilson College, Chambersburg, PA; her M.S. in Child and Family Studies from St. Cloud State University in St. Cloud, MN; and her Ph.D. in Curriculum and Instruction from the University of Minnesota. She is an assistant professor in the Department of Child and Family Studies at St. Cloud State University, where she has taught since 1988. In addition to multiage grouping, her research interests have been concentrated around diversity and antibiased education. She is a consultant for the early childhood education community on those topics and has done extensive antiracism training with European-Americans.

Jill Anderson is an elementary classroom teacher in Cambridge, Minnesota. After teaching for 15 years in a traditional, age-segregated classroom, she helped initiate the development and implementation of a multiage program for children in her school. Believing that developmental learning happens most naturally in settings that encourage daily interaction between children of different ages, she is eager to share her perspective of the multiage experience. She is currently completing her master's degree and conducting research on self-regulating behavior in multiage classrooms. In addition to teaching full-time, she actively collaborates with a network of multi-age teachers in neighboring school districts. She has been a presenter, both formally and informally, in several schools and at regional conferences. Along with coauthors Nancy Bacharach and Robin Christine Hasslen, she recently presented multiage research findings at the 1994 American Educational Research Association Conference.

This book is dedicated to:

David, Kimberly, and Megan
With all my love.
N.B.

Joel, Jessica, and Tom
who stand by through all my endeavors.
R.H.

Jim, Jenny, and Mike
Many thanks for your love and support!
J.A.

ONE

What Is Multiage Grouping?

Case Study: The Student's Perspective

Jeremy begins his school day on the bus. He greets his neighbors and friends and proceeds to sit with a classmate. During the 35-minute ride to school, Jeremy discusses the new theme recently started in his multiage classroom at McMaster Elementary. It is a sports theme, and he is excited to share the baseball card collection that he carefully holds on his lap. Jeremy, at 8 years old, is aware that he has both the opportunity and the responsibility to contribute to the learning of his classmates. By carefully labeling and categorizing his collection according to team names, Jeremy is ready to share. Because his mom is at work, Jeremy's grandpa is going to stop by the elementary school at 1 p.m. to watch Jeremy's presentation. Various members of Jeremy's family have come to school regularly throughout the year. This has been encouraged and soundly supported by his teachers as an important way to link home and school. Because this is Jeremy's second year in this multiage program, he has a real sense that his parent and teachers are working together to help him achieve the goals he helped set at the beginning of the school year.

Jeremy arrives at school and proceeds to his homeroom, where he places his card collection on the display table. While offering a wave and smile to his conference teacher, Mrs. Anderson, he stops by the attendance and lunch count chart to check himself in for the day. Jeremy is learning to make good decisions and heads to the library to check out the Matt Christopher book

1

*he will need for Literature Circle later today. He asks his study buddy, Alan,
a 6-year-old in the same classroom, if he would like to go along. Alan has
forgotten all about the literature assignment and happily goes with Jeremy,
feeling more confident about school and learning because Jeremy is there to help.*

The Definition of Multiage Grouping

Defined most basically, multiage grouping, in which Jeremy and
Alan participate, describes a classroom purposefully composed of
children who are more than 1 year apart in age. Such grouping is
random, rather than selective. For example, classrooms do not con-
sist of the most advanced first graders in combination with the least
advanced second graders. The rationale for multiage grouping is
based on meeting students' individual needs. This rationale, rather
than bureaucratic budget concerns, is the driving force behind multiage classrooms. The groupings are not determined by financial
constraints that might dictate combining several ages in order to
alleviate the need for an additional teacher, textbooks, or classroom
space. Rather, students are grouped together across ages in combi-
nations most beneficial to their educational stimulation and success.

Common terms associated with nontraditional groupings include *mixed-age, heterogeneous, vertical, family, continuous progress,* and
ungraded or nongraded. However, Katz has distinguished between
nongraded and multiaged classrooms by defining the former's rationale and format as ability grouping, and the latter's as interaction
among children of different ages (Katz, Evangelou, & Hartman,
1990). Although many people use these terms interchangeably, for
the purposes of this book and in recognition of the above distinction,
the term *multiage* will be used consistently.

Our families, neighborhoods, and communities are all multiage
learning environments, yet the composition of most schools today
does not reflect the natural groupings found in the world. Multiage
classrooms, as representations of these environments, provide opportunities for the exchange of ideas, modeling of behaviors, practice
of responsibility and nurturance, and development of leadership
and social skills.

There are a number of basic principles and practices that under-
lie multiage classrooms:

1. developmentally appropriate curricula and practices
2. active, child-centered, and continuous learning
3. attention to the education of the whole child
4. the teacher as facilitator
5. integrated curriculum across subjects
6. the absence of rigid instructional strategies and assessments (American Association of School Administrators, 1992).

These characteristics will be discussed throughout the book.

A developmental, child-centered philosophy of learning guides multiage classroom practices. Teachers utilize various strategies, such as cooperative learning, peer tutoring, self-directed and experience-based learning, and/or the whole-language approach with theme-related activities (see Chapter 3). The sports theme in Jeremy's classroom allowed him to take charge of his learning. Because of his personal interest in baseball cards, he was eager to organize and categorize his collection. This is an example of self-directed learning typical of multiage classroom students. Jeremy also provided an excellent role model for Alan and demonstrated the peer tutoring interaction intrinsic to multiage classrooms.

The Need for Multiage Grouping

The world of the 1990s is complex. Technological changes, increased mobility, alternative family structures, and growing ethnic populations are contributing to a society that is constantly changing and increasingly diverse and demanding. For an individual to survive and be a contributing member of society, he or she will need to adapt to such changes and diversity. Like Jeremy, today's children hold memberships in families whose structures are no longer defined by two parents and numerous siblings. The families are more mobile and the marriages less stable. The population is composed of increasingly fewer European-Americans and greater numbers of individuals representing other ethnic groups.

Such complexity demands appropriate and sensitive interactions, which in turn require a solid educational base. The task of education is to prepare children not merely to be survivors in society, but also to be positive contributors. This task has remained the same throughout the years; however, the population of students has changed. Today's school children are diverse by family structure and functioning, ethnicity, race, ability, and early experiences. It is this complexity, rather than any philosophy, that warrants and should motivate educational systems to accommodate students who are reflecting the diversity in society (Goodlad & Anderson, 1987). Multiage grouping celebrates diversity and values the richness of different perspectives, backgrounds, and experiences. In examining multiage grouping, Cushman (1990, p. 30) suggests, "By creating a model that expects diversity rather than uniformity among kids, many of the 'problems' in a single grade class lose their destructive grip over teachers and students both." On the other hand, some teachers in traditional classroom groupings value homogeneity and the ease inherent in teaching students who are similar.

Today's students enter classrooms typically programmed for homogeneity, not for heterogeneity. Regardless of what the child brings into the preschool or elementary school setting, he or she is expected to conform to the demands of the structured environment and inflexible curriculum, rather than having his or her needs met. Yet we know that children learn at different rates in different ways.

Typically, schools provide lists of requirements for success in kindergarten. Multiage groupings ease the parents' burden of responsibility for determining when their children are ready for learning. This is accomplished through the individualizing of curricula and instruction. Research has proven that failure at an early age, such as that involving kindergarten retention, is damaging to young children's esteem and excitement about education (Katz & Chard, 1989; Shepard & Smith, 1990). Multiage grouping eliminates the need for retention, and enhances children's self-esteem and excitement about learning (see Chapter 2).

The Multiage Setting

Traditional classroom organization of students by chronological age and/or ability does not adequately address the characteristics and needs of many of today's school children. Teacher-directed learning, tracking, and grade retention are distinctive features of many of these classrooms. Consistent with such homogeneous group-ings are narrow definitions of academic ability and performance criteria for evaluation. An alternative configuration, which groups students who span more than 1 year in age, seeks to optimize learning by individualizing instruction and maximizing children's interaction. Multiage grouping, by virtue of its classroom composi-tion, must rely on developmentally appropriate, individually and culturally relevant practices. In Jeremy's case, his enthusiasm for the baseball card collection motivated him to continue his exploration of the sports theme by seeking sports-related literature in the library.

Curriculum and instructional strategies that are individualized and child-centered have been labeled "developmentally appropriate practices" by the National Association for the Education of Young Children (NAEYC) (Bredekamp, 1987). Such practices assume that a wide range of developmental differences exist among any group of children, and provide for those varying abilities, interests, and skills without limiting learning to grade level expectations. Developmen-tally appropriate practices form the foundation for multiage class-rooms.

The History of Multiage Grouping

Although the purpose of this book does not focus on the history of multiage grouping, it is always important to take a brief look into the history of any educational phenomenon, to learn from the past. Most American children attend schools organized by separate grade levels, with grade placement largely determined by age. At the age of 5, children enter kindergarten with all the other 5-year-olds. However, in the early 19th century, most of our schools consisted of one teacher working with students at a variety of ages. There were 196,037 one-room schools in existence in 1918 (Muse, Smith, & Barker, 1987). These one-room schoolhouses typically accommo-dated 10 to 30 students, ranging in age from 6 to 14. The solitary teacher delivered instruction individually for approximately two 20-minute periods a day to each child (Goodlad & Anderson, 1987). This grouping of students was a direct result of geographic and economic factors and had little, if anything, to do with the philoso-phy that surrounds multiage grouping today.

One of the major forces in moving away from one-room school-houses toward gradedness was 19th-century educational leader Horace Mann. After a visit to German schools, Mann, Secretary of the Board of Education of Massachusetts, maintained "the first element of superiority consists of proper classification of scholars" (Mann, 1970, p. 84). A number of other factors also led to age segregation in schools. Public, state-supported education increased the number of students coming to school. This education of the masses created a need for an economical and efficient model of education. Graded schools were born out of administrative practicality, rather than any sound educational research base providing support for this structure.

Another strong factor in the move toward gradedness was the publication of graded texts. In 1821 Warren Colburn produced a modern set of arithmetic texts, followed in 1836 by the McGuffey Eclectic Readers (Goodlad & Anderson, 1987). Other graded texts in various content fields emerged and became the expected norms for grade levels. Legislation followed, mandating standardized age at entry into school and sequential grade levels and curriculum.

In 1848 the Quincy Grammar School, in Boston, opened its doors, showcasing a new organizational pattern of grouping students according to age. Many predicted then that this new design would set the stage for 50 years to come (Goodlad & Anderson, 1987). By 1860 graded schools were widely adopted, especially in large cities. More than 140 years later, our nation's schools still adhere to the basic structure of gradedness. As Goodlad and Anderson (1963) so eloquently state, "graded schools became not a landmark, but a shrine" (p. 204). The one-room schoolhouse survived mainly in rural areas where the population did not support an age-segregated model. By 1980 there were fewer than 1,000 one-room schools in America (Muse et al., 1987).

A number of isolated efforts to move away from a graded model for public education took place in the 20th century. John Dewey's lab school at the University of Chicago challenged the established practice by eliminating the arbitrary placement of students into grades according to age. Many examine the open education movement of the 1960s as a move away from the typical graded structure. Individually Guided Education (IGE), a hallmark of the open era, was an approach that combined team teaching, multiage grouping, and nongraded classrooms. These attempts at moving away from the graded structure were isolated events and were not widely replicated.

Amidst national calls for fundamental educational reform, multiage grouping has once again emerged as an organizational structure worth pursuing. The states of Kentucky and Oregon, along with the Canadian province of British Columbia, have mandated ungraded primary schools (Gaustad, 1992). New literature examining the effectiveness of multiage grouping is emerging as many schools across the nation make the decision to use a multiage model.

SUMMARY

The population in the United States today is diverse; there is no argument about that. In light of changing demographics, there should also be no argument about the need for restructuring in education. Multiage grouping has been one alternative for a structure which is developmentally and individually appropriate. Although the configuration of multiage grouping is not new to this country, the rationale for its utilization today is different. We are not grouping students out of financial or geographic necessity, but from a basic philosophical belief that such a structure is beneficial for optimal growth and education.

TWO

Why Use Multiage Grouping?

Case Study: The Teacher's Perspective

Six first- and second-grade teachers are sitting at a table in one of their classrooms in McMaster Elementary School. They are debating the pros and cons of a multiage classroom. Ms. Kemper, a first-grade teacher, begins by asking, "But why in the world would I want to have a larger range of abilities in my classroom? I already find it difficult to meet everyone's needs!"

Ms. Jenison agrees, "All of my materials and curriculum revolve around first grade. I wouldn't know what to do with second graders."

"I understand your feelings," interjects Mr. Gannon. "I don't have a clue about how to work with a room full of first graders who don't know how to read or write!"

"Well," says Ms. Johnson, "Aren't you both already dealing with those issues? Not all of your first graders 'fit' the first-grade curriculum, and you are constantly making adaptations. And Jim, you have second graders who come to you unable to read and write; you deal with them!"

"I think we need to explore why we might want to move in this direction," adds Mr. Tiffen. "I mean, what does the research say? How do we know multiage grouping will work?"

"That's a good point," says Ms. Johnson. "Let's do some reading about the rationale behind multiage grouping."

The Theories Behind Multiage Grouping

The foundation for multiage grouping is rooted in a number of theoretical and philosophical frameworks with respect to child development and education. Children grow and develop at different rates, separate and distinct from each other but interrelated with their environment. Teachers, such as the six teachers at McMaster Elementary, need to be aware of the theoretical support for multiage grouping so that curricula and pedagogy that are consistent with the concept's philosophy can be developed. Multiage grouping is based on some principles from the following theories: cognitive, social learning, sociocultural, psychosocial, and ecological.

Cognitive Theory

Piaget, a developmental psychologist, hypothesized that children must have opportunities to interact with their environment in order to develop. Such interaction enables them to construct knowledge. Thus, to Piaget (1973), learning was a dynamic process, with individuals as active constructors of their own development. Piaget believed that the social environment's role in a child's development was as important as that of the physical environment, with each relationship playing a role in shaping the individual. In a multiage group setting, students are constantly adding to their knowledge bases, broadening their perspectives, and developing their social skills through increased opportunities to interact with one another.

Learning, according to cognitive developmentalists, in addition to being experiential, is also maturational. Piaget would find merit in teaching strategies and curricula that are individualized enough for children to learn according to their cognitive developmental level. The multiage classroom is designed to provide students with opportunities to interact, as their interests dictate, with both the physical and the social environments.

Ms. Johnson, a teacher in this chapter's case study, was correct when she reminded the other teachers that in reality they are adapting their curricula all the time. And if they are not making adaptations, they are probably not meeting individual needs. A multiage grouping *demands* that teachers individualize content and strategies.

Social Learning Theory

Cognitive theorists view social learning as a product of development dependent on the child's interactions and stage of intellectual development. Social learning theorists see development as the product of social learning. Thus, development is affected through observation and imitation of and identification with others. Children think, feel, and act based on their expectations and motives. They form perceptions and attitudes out of a need to organize their environments. Bandura, a social learning theorist, described the cognitive aspect of children's learning as a continuous reciprocal interaction between individuals and their environments. Through observations, children acquire new responses to add to future behavioral repertoires. Bandura (1977) proposed that observation as a method of learning is more efficient than a trial-and-error method and provides examples of more complex behaviors that are not easily learned through other means. Multiage classrooms provide a multiplicity of opportunities for younger children to emulate older children. Studies on positive social effects of multiage grouping (i.e., enhancement of social skills, leadership, cooperation, etc.) substantiate Bandura's position on the impact of interactions on children's development.

Sociocultural Theory

Vygotsky (1978), a Russian psychologist, also focused on the social aspect of children's learning through guidance and examples of others. However, he also stressed the importance of understanding the expectations, tools, skills, and interactions provided by a child's culture. The term *zone of proximal development* has been defined by Vygotsky to describe "the distance between the actual developmental level as determined by independent problem solving and the level of potential development as determined through problem solving under adult guidance or in collaboration with more capable peers" (p. 86). Peers in multiage classrooms can facilitate development by assisting children in moving to the next level of understanding. The heterogeneity present in a multiage classroom can also provide a variety of tools, skills, and methods of interaction that are culturally appropriate.

Psychosocial Theory

The child's social environment is also emphasized in the work of Erik Erikson (1950), whose psychosocial theory proposed that individuals face a series of psychological and social challenges as they develop. Success or failure in resolving the psychosocial conflicts of each stage of development is determined by the individuals' relationships and by demands placed on them by society. During the stages from early through middle childhood, children face the conflicts of autonomy versus shame or doubt, initiative versus guilt, and industry versus inferiority.

Although each of these stages differs in emphasis, each entails positive and negative characteristics that can be affected by school environments. Multiage relationships can also serve to affect the resolutions of these stage conflicts. For example, in multiage settings, students practice autonomy through their self-directed learning and problem-solving opportunities. Initiative and industry are traits enhanced by students' feelings of success, as measured by authentic activities and achievements rather than standardized assessments.

Ecological Theory

Bronfenbrenner (1989) has viewed the environment as a nested system of interrelationships. From the individual through the community, society, and world, the impact of interactions has a rippling effect. Development is the result of those interrelationships. For example, a child's education is affected by family support, community tax base, and societal emphasis. A child in a multiage classroom is a product of his or her home, peer relationships, community, broader society, and country. Thus, what the child brings into the classroom in terms of abilities, interests, cultural values, and beliefs will be unique. A necessary continuity between school and home is made possible in a school setting that more closely represents a diverse world. Multiage classrooms, because of their diverse make-up, reflect the reality of the world.

This wide range of theoretical viewpoints provides a solid groundwork for the concept of multiage grouping. It is upon such a base that educators should begin to build a structure that meets

Theory	Theorist	Application
Cognitive Development	J. Piaget	* Children are active constructors of knowledge.
Social Learning	A. Bandura	* Development is the product of social learning, through observation, imitation, identification with others.
Sociocultural	L. S. Vygotsky	* "Zone of proximal development" is the distance between actual and potential developmental levels and is facilitated by collaboration with others.
Psychosocial	E. Erikson	* Individuals face a series of psychological and social challenges, the success of which is largely determined by relationships and societal demands.
Ecological	U. Bronfenbrenner	* Development is the result of interrelationships of child and all levels of society.

Figure 2.1. The Theories Behind Multiage Grouping

the needs of a large segment of today's student population. Ms. Johnson and Mr. Tiffen were correct in recognizing their need to study the rationale for multiage grouping before moving in that direction.

The Research Base
Underlying Multiage Grouping

Educational Practices

The National Association for the Education of Young Children (NAEYC) has proposed that educators follow practices that are both developmentally and individually appropriate for young children. Such practices involve: (a) hands-on learning through play and exploration; (b) activities that meet the needs of wide ranges of ability and interest levels; (c) responsive teacher-pupil relationships that are sensitive to the needs, interests, and readiness of the whole child; and (d) child-centered environments that demand problem-solving, student interactions, and the enhancement of creative and critical thinking (Bredekamp, 1987). Multiage grouping reflects the NAEYC guidelines for educational practices that are developmentally appropriate.

Lillian Katz (Katz, Evangelou, & Hartman, 1990) has proposed that multiage grouping be an essential part of early childhood education because it resembles the traditional, natural family and neighborhood groupings. Even at the preschool level, multiage grouping enhances social development and enables children to stimulate each others' social and cognitive growth. Katz also finds merit in multiage grouping's means of measuring progress, which reduces the need to screen and utilize standardized tests with young children.

The Department of Elementary-Kindergarten-Nursery Education (1968) has described the values of multiage grouping to include: (a) each child learning through social interaction; (b) more cooperation than competition; (c) greater opportunities for children to gain more insight into human striving, initiating, and imitating; (d) acquisition of human skills of helpfulness, concern, and giving; and (e) the acquisition of greater security by older children in interactions with younger children.

In *The Process of Education*, Jerome Bruner (1960) begins with the following premise:

Each generation gives new form to the aspirations that shape education in its time. What may be emerging as a mark of

our own generation is a widespread renewal of concern for
the quality and intellectual aims of education—but without
abandonment of the ideal that education should serve as a
means of training well-balanced citizens for a democracy. (p. 1)

Although Bruner is not addressing the concept of multiage
grouping, his philosophy fits the multiage model. An example of
Bruner's educational theory is the importance of students' learning
of structure, or the general idea behind a skill or concept, followed
by the students' broadening and deepening of knowledge. Educators in a multiage classroom must be aware of children's readiness
for learning and then provide education appropriate to the child's
stage of development. Utilization of a spiral curriculum, one that
builds on earlier concepts, enables students to acquire and manipulate new information, and also challenges them to advance beyond
their present dealings with the information. Of importance to Bruner
is the students' interest in learning and acquisition of appropriate
attitudes and values about intellectual activity. Multiage classrooms
promote spiral curricula as well as intellectual curiosity and excitement.

In a summary of cross-cultural research on grouping patterns,
Freedman (1981) determined that groupings reflect the goals of the
programs:

Where the primary goal is to produce open, sociable children
who are able to accept and give help, heterogeneous grouping is preferred. Where the goal is to teach a set body of
material and to formalize the relationship between depen-
dents and caregivers, homogeneous grouping is favored. (p. 9)

Students in multiage groups gain not only knowledge but self-
esteem and social skills such as empathy, responsibility, leadership,
cooperation, and so on.

Research in the area of multiage grouping has been hampered
by the lack of a clear vision of the concept. However, the most
definitive evidence for benefits of such grouping points to the following: (a) improvement of language skills; (b) greater success for
students at developmental extremes, males, and low-income students; (c) increased self-esteem; (d) a rise in achievement scores

following longer stays in multiage classrooms; (e) the fostering of social development; and (f) the increased personalism of teachers and their willingness to individualize education (Cushman, 1990).

In short, educational research has revealed that multiage grouping enhances social development, and for many students, cognitive development as well.

Social Effects

Studies of children's social perceptions in multiage groups reveal that children associate specific expectations with specific age groups. Younger children assign roles of leadership and skills of instruction, assistance, and sympathizing to older children, and older children perceive younger students in need of help and instruction (French, 1984). Such perceptions tend to create a climate of cooperation that is beneficial to both younger and older children. It has been noted that there often exists increased competition and aggression among same-age peers (Hartup, 1979), and increased harmony and nurturance within multiage groups (Wakefield, 1979). Studies have found older children exhibiting leadership roles in mixed-age groups (French, Waas, Stright, & Baker, 1986; Stright & French, 1988).

Reviewing a number of studies, Buckholdt and Wodarski (1978) concluded that multiage preschool groupings, in which children are allowed to occasionally serve as teacher, promoted interpersonal and cooperative skills, social perspectives, role-taking, and empathy. Social interaction in the form of leadership skills was studied by Mobley (1976), who found improvement in the self-concepts of students in grades 1 to 3 in multiage settings but no noticeable improvement in homogeneous settings. Sociability was found to be enhanced in mixed-age groupings with children interacting more frequently with peers than adults (Goldman, 1981; Reuter & Yunik, 1973).

Prosocial behavior has also been found to be enhanced within mixed-age groups. Graziano, French, Brownell, and Hartup (1976) found first and third graders to be more sensitive to complex interactions inherent in multiage settings. Positive, spontaneous attention to peers, plus affection and reciprocation, are traits demonstrated in multiage settings (Lougee, Grueneich, & Hartup, 1977).

Older children's self-regulation has been found to improve when they remind younger children of rules (Lougee & Graziano, 1986). The multiage classroom atmosphere fosters more cooperation and less competition, thus reducing discipline problems. Roopnarine (1987) found that younger children in multiage groups were able to participate in more complex play situations when more competent children initiated the situation.

Attitudes Toward School and Self-Concept

Evidence points to children's ability to learn from each other (Pratt, 1983; Whiting, 1983; Whiting & Edwards, 1988). Children learn from each other both in cooperative group situations and in one-on-one encounters as they learn from each other's various perspectives and experiences. "The evidence on multiage grouping appears to confirm the basic principle that diversity enriches and uniformity impoverishes" (Pratt, 1983, p. 114).

In a study of therapeutic effects of multiage grouping, Furman, Rahe, and Hartup (1979) found that withdrawn preschoolers' interaction with younger children enhanced the former's social skills of leadership and sociability. Younger children who are experiencing social difficulties have also been found to benefit from cross-age interaction (Kim, 1990). Carbone (1961/62) reported that children in nongraded schools had more positive attitudes about their teachers. They were described as big, quiet, interesting, soft, bright, smooth, sweet, relaxed, and good, as compared to graded schools where teachers were described as little, loud, boring, hard, dull, rough, sour, stiff, and bad.

Utilizing the Piers-Harris Children's Self-Concept Scale in a study of elementary multiage and traditional classrooms, Way (1981) found significant differences on the factor of Happiness and Satisfaction. Results showed students in multiage classrooms to demonstrate a more positive score than those from traditional classrooms.

Cognitive Development

Brown and Palincsar (1986) found that children's mixed-age interactions can result in cognitive conflict, or intellectual discord, which leads to cognitive growth. Slavin's (1987) research on coop-

Research has provided evidence that multiage classrooms:

1. Promote and value diversity (Kim, 1990).

2. Promote cooperative rather than competitive behavior (French, 1984; Howes & Farver, 1987).

3. Increase children's social skills and industry (French et al., 1986; Howes & Farver, 1987; Stright & French, 1988).

4. Enhance children's altruistic behaviors (Buckholdt & Wodarski, 1978; Graziano et al., 1976; Lougee et al., 1977).

5. Accommodate differently abled children (Freedman, 1981; Johnson & Johnson, 1987).

6. Expand children's age-range of friends and interactive learning (Goldman, 1981; Mounts & Roopnarine, 1987; Pratt, 1983; Whiting, 1983; Whiting & Edwards, 1988).

7. Provide for consistent teacher/pupil relationships, and thereby feelings of trust and security (Carbone, 1961/62).

8. Enhance self-concept (Hammack, 1975; Mobley, 1976; Way, 1981).

9. Promote greater sociability (Goldman, 1981; Reuter & Yunik, 1973).

10. Promote greater problem-solving skills (Azmitia, 1988).

Figure 2.2. Social Advantages of Multiage Grouping

erative learning has revealed that individuals can grow cognitively through cooperative efforts. Multiage students spend a great deal of time working in cooperative groups and have considerable opportunity to learn from each other.

Problem-solving ability has been found to be enhanced within multiage settings when older children offer information, guidance, and new viewpoints, and demonstrate social skills such as negotiation, argumentation, and cooperative work skills (Azmitia, 1988). Younger children in mixed-age groups have been shown to develop such language skills as sentence length and complexity by the children's adjusting their communication for each other (Gelman & Baillargeon, 1983; Lougee et al., 1977; Shatz & Gelman, 1973).

Pratt (1983) concluded, from a review of research on age segregation in schools, that

> in one sense, the evidence on age composition of instructional groups vindicates the conventional assumption that what is most natural is most educative. Reflection on the evidence suggests that there is nothing natural about age segregation. A natural learning group, like a natural social group, is one in which a commonality of interest and a shared readiness for a task is complemented by a diversity of age and other characteristics. If schools could approach this ideal, they might become more natural and more educative places. (p. 31)

SUMMARY

Through this brief analysis of theories and research, it can be seen that multiage grouping has evolved from a broad theoretical base. Evidence for the rationale underlying the multiage concept has been procured from numerous theories. It is exciting to find that principles gleaned from a variety of theoretical constructs all support the necessity for individualized and child-directed learning. Children learn in ways that are not always predictable in terms of a developmental timetable. This is borne out by both theory and research.

Although current research provides convincing evidence as to the necessity of and justification for this educational model, most attention is directed to the social aspects of multiage grouping. What perhaps should become more of a focus is the interrelationship between a child's psychological/emotional self and his or her ability to develop cognitively. Meanwhile, there is a great need for continued study of the multiage concept.

THREE

What Does Multiage Grouping Look Like?

Case Study: The Administrator's Perspective

The telephone rings in Principal Clarke's office at McMaster Elementary School. . . .

"Ms. Clarke, are you able to take a call from a parent wanting information on the multiage unit? It seems that Mr. Jones, Susie's dad, is confused about the changes taking place here at the school."

"I am in a meeting right now with two teachers," Ms. Clarke responds, "please take his number; I'll call him back shortly."

Ms. Clarke turns back to her conversation with two very dedicated, caring teachers and explains how multiage grouping can be beneficial to children. "In truth," she states, "you must ask yourself two simple questions: (1) How do children learn? and (2) How do teachers teach?" The two veteran teachers agree, but then begin to voice their frustrations:

"The textbooks we're using do not support this type of programming. Don't we have an obligation to follow the mandates of our district curriculum committees?"

"Our middle school colleagues are up in arms. They are concerned that multiage grouping at the elementary level will drastically affect their middle school programming in the near future."

"We've seen many concepts and reforms come and go over the years. What if multiage grouping doesn't have staying power?"

Ms. Clarke agrees that the barriers sometimes seem insurmountable. She stresses the importance of a child-centered curriculum taught in a natural, flexible environment that ensures students' learning and success. Ms. Clark reminds her teachers of an in-service she is providing for parents and teachers next week on multiage classrooms. She encourages them to give it more thought and to stay open to the ideas. As the teachers leave the office, Principal Clark picks up the phone to return Mr. Jones's call and invite him to the same in-service.

Program Components

Although Principal Clarke is aware that communication is key to implementing change, she is *most* interested in creating a climate in which conversation about children and learning can occur. Helping her teachers develop a "like mind" philosophy is paramount to beginning the transition from conventional, graded classroom structures to multiage group settings. An unsuccessful attempt at multiage grouping is often the result of shallow belief systems on the part of teachers, administrators, and parents. It is imperative that healthy discussions about "why we do what we do" happen before any change occurs.

As schools move into exploring multiage grouping as a potential educational option, a frequent question is, "What does it look like?" Successful implementation of a multiage program involves a careful examination of a number of schools, followed by the creation of a unique model to fit the specific needs of a particular site. It is unwise to simply replicate an existing model and expect it to work. It would be much simpler if *the* model could be dictated, but as with any structural pattern, it must be custom-built to meet the specific needs that exist.

There are numerous variables, including the community, school, teachers, parents, and students, that must be taken into consideration before a multiage model is implemented. The only element common across every multiage classroom is the intentional grouping of children of more than one traditional grade level into one classroom. Because multiage grouping is a structure that allows a move away from prescribed, predetermined curricula, instruction, and assessment, each classroom, school, and district must develop the model that works for their particular situation. There are, however, certain elements that typically appear in multiage classrooms. These elements can be classified into three common areas: Beliefs, Curricular and Instructional Elements, and Assessment Elements.

Beliefs

Our traditional model of age grouping in school assumes that when children reach a specific age, they will all automatically possess the same physical, mental, social, and intellectual abilities. Not only is this not true, we wouldn't *want* it to be. However, we have developed graded curricula that all but our students with identified special needs must complete. For example, we maintain that we value individuality, yet we try to fit all 6-year-olds into one mold—a first-grade mold. As teachers, if we find that a student does not fit into the mold, we look for additional resources—materials, aides, time—to get the student to fit into the mold.

One of the premises of multiage grouping is that we value diversity and we demonstrate this by throwing out the mold. There is no prepackaged, predetermined curriculum that will meet all of our students' needs. Instead, the focus is on the individual child. First we must examine where the child is, and then we design curriculum and instruction to meet the child's needs. Learning is hands-on and activity-based. Because of the diversity within the classroom, a single set of expectations for learners becomes an absurd goal. A discrete set of facts in any subject area is replaced by a focus on the process of learning. Students are not spoon-fed material but instead become self-regulating, self-directed learners.

Curricular and Instructional Elements

Graded textbooks, used heavily in traditional classrooms, are used as only one resource in a multiage classroom. Graded textbooks propagate the idea of conformity and tend to be stumbling blocks for teachers implementing individualized instruction. Much of the curriculum and instruction that occurs in a multiage classroom must be created as the students develop a need for it. There are no absolutes in adopting particular curricular and instructional elements when moving into a multiage setting. There are, however, a number of elements that lend themselves well to the diversity that exists and is celebrated in a multiage classroom. These elements include, but are not limited to, process writing, literature-based reading, thematic teaching, learning centers, math manipulatives, cooperative learning, peer tutoring, computer-assisted instruction, and team teaching.

Process Writing

Process writing is an approach to teaching writing that focuses on valuing and learning the processes that are a part of writing, instead of focusing on a product (Calkins, 1988; Graves, 1983). This model is a natural fit in a multiage classroom because it allows for differences in abilities and interests. For instance, all children may be writing about the rain forest, but the process and product of each student will be different. As writing takes place there may be children at the picture-writing level, where they will simply be drawing a picture to represent a thought or story; others will be at a scribble-writing phase, which involves attempts at making shapes that approximate letters. Some students in the same classroom will be using the random letter phase as others go through the invented spelling phase. Last, there will be students reaching the conventional writing phase, in which they will spell most words correctly. All students then, can be involved in writing, working, and progressing at their individual developmental levels.

Literature-Based Reading

Literature-based reading is an approach that uses children's literature and a wide range of reading materials to teach reading (Wiseman, 1992). Materials used in this approach are written to be read for enjoyment, as opposed to texts that are written exclusively for instruction. Children are given chunks of class time to read, and instruction is geared to individual interests and abilities. The premise is that children participate in real reading for real purposes, emulating the types of things mature readers do.

In a multiage classroom, literature-based reading allows for children to be reading at their own level as opposed to having everyone in the same text. For example, everyone may be reading about dinosaurs, but advanced readers will be reading more complex texts than the emerging readers. In a literature-based classroom, children respond to text in varied ways. Rather than completing workbook pages after reading a story, a child might create a puppet show, a book jacket, or a song about the story. This allows for the diversity of interests and skills we find in all classrooms.

Learning Centers

Learning centers include collections of materials and activities ranging from concrete to abstract. Students interact with the centers to learn, reinforce, or apply concepts. Because learning centers provide a variety of stimuli, they tend to meet the diverse learning styles and abilities within a classroom. For instance, a teacher may set up a learning center relating to electricity. A variety of materials, such as books, writing materials, batteries, light bulbs, and wire, would allow the students to explore electricity by utilizing either concrete and/or abstract thinking. Learning centers also provide an opportunity for students to interact, collaborate, and participate in an active, hands-on format.

Math Manipulatives

Math manipulatives are concrete materials and activities with which students interact to better understand a mathematical concept. Consistent use of math manipulatives gives students regular opportunities to demonstrate and construct relationships with objects before moving into symbols. Students are encouraged to construct their own arrangements, groupings, patterns, and relationships. Students create and recognize patterns in their world by building and creating interesting designs with pattern blocks and unifix cubes. This is a preliminary step to creating and recognizing number patterns. Students recognize similarities and differences by collecting and organizing buttons, blocks, or beans. This is a preliminary step to classifying.

Sand timers, sequencing cards, and pictures prepare students to understand the concept of time. Paper clip chains, strings, and body measures such as hand spans prepare children to understand the concept of measurement. The study of mathematics has traditionally been limited to paper-and-pencil activities with an emphasis on correct answers. This approach incorrectly assumes a student's understanding of the process involved in mathematical concepts. Using manipulatives is a logical step toward developing a truer understanding. These hands-on, process-oriented activities fit well into a multiage classroom.

Cooperative Learning

Cooperative learning is a collection of strategies designed to foster interdependence among learners. Cooperative learning focuses on minimizing the competition found in most classrooms. Competition tends to discourage students from helping each other (Slavin, 1990). Cooperative learning strategies are designed to facilitate students working together to reach a common goal. The collaborative, group consensus, supportive learning that occurs in cooperative groups reflects the skills and attitudes the children will need to contribute to society as adults. Kohn (1992) suggests that success in the workplace includes teamwork, getting along with others, and shared decision making. Cognitive development and the use of critical thinking strategies are promoted through peer interaction (Slavin, 1990). The type of environment created through cooperative learning honors the diversity of individuals present in a multiage classroom and supports the concept of social learning.

Thematic Teaching

Choosing a central theme that is the focus throughout the various content areas during a school day is called thematic teaching. Thematic teaching allows children to explore a particular topic in depth from multiple disciplines. Ties between content areas are made explicit and children read, write, and respond to a topic in a variety of forums. Theme teaching provides the opportunity to create an environment that supports and encourages process learning (Thompson, 1991). In a multiage classroom, theme teaching allows all students to share a common concept, yet provides the opportunity for each child to work on that concept at the appropriate developmental level.

Peer Tutoring

Students helping other students is the basis of peer tutoring. With the range of abilities in a classroom, peer tutoring allows for the more advanced student to assist the emerging learner in any area of the curriculum. Peer tutoring can be beneficial for all students and has been shown to enhance both the tutor and the tutee's academic performance. In addition, peer tutoring enhances self-esteem and confidence and leads to better social relationships and more positive attitudes (Topping, 1988). Further, tutees often grasp material more readily when it is presented by a peer. In addition, tutees are provided with excellent models to emulate.

Computer-Assisted Instruction

Computer-assisted instruction (CAI) enables a concept to be taught, practiced, applied, or reinforced by utilizing a computer program. Computers can provide individualized instruction by automatically allowing students to work at their own pace. For instance, in studying fractions, one student may work on a computer program that teaches basic understanding of the concept while another student is solving application problems related to the same concept. In addition to gaining some of the basic technological competencies necessary for the future, students tend to find interaction with computers stimulating. The fast-paced, interactive characteristics of computers, along with the creative and colorful programs that provide immediate feedback, grab the attention of learners.

Team Teaching

Team teaching can be defined as two or more teachers simultaneously responsible for an entire educational program for a group of students (Broadby, 1982). In comparison, traditional teaching is typically an isolated activity. Team teaching provides collegial support for teachers. Most teachers working in teams find it exciting and feel they maintain higher levels of energy and creativity.

Assessment

Assessment is an area of concern that has generated heated debate across the country. According to Farr (1992), "The bottom line in selecting and using any assessment should be whether it helps students" (p. 28). Traditionally, schools have used what R. Anderson (1993) calls "competitive-comparative pupil evaluation systems" (p. 9). This method of assessment typically utilizes standardized and/or formalized tests that assume there is one right answer. The tests focus on the product and do little to measure the process of learning that is emphasized in a multiage classroom.

In addition, formalized testing tends to assess children on their conformity and does not celebrate the diversity inherent in classrooms. Although standardized/formalized testing may be a rough indicator of student progress, it does little to guide teachers in creating developmentally appropriate curricula. For assessment to be optimally valuable to teachers and students, it must be embedded in the curriculum. Hence, a teacher in a multiage classroom must consider alternatives and additions to standardized/formalized testing.

As is the case with any classroom teacher, multiage teachers must begin the assessment process by determining the essential student competencies. For example, the Cambridge Multiage program (see Chapter 4) has the following outcomes:

1. The learner demonstrates the ability to communicate thoughts and ideas orally.
2. The learner demonstrates the ability to communicate thoughts and ideas in written form.
3. The learner reads for understanding.
4. The learner develops a "number sense" to organize mathematical concepts.
5. The learner develops an awareness of the benefits and purposes of technology.

6. The learner uses the scientific process during experiences with physical, chemical, biological, and earth sciences.

7. The learner recognizes different behaviors and the many factors that influence the way people act, live, and learn.

8. The learner develops skills necessary to function as an independent learner.

9. The learner recognizes the importance of maintaining good health.

10. The learner develops an understanding and appreciation for art, music, and drama. (Cambridge Elementary MAG Program, 1991)

Once the program outcomes are delineated, curriculum and instruction are determined and multiple indicators of attainment are utilized. Although these basic assessment concepts apply to most classrooms, there are additional issues specific to a multiage setting. Due to the diverse learning needs and styles within a multiage classroom, assessment must be done on an individual level. The use of portfolios in multiage classrooms appears to fit the need for flexible, individualized, ongoing assessment. A second very important component of assessment involves teacher/student/parent conferences.

Portfolios

Portfolios are a collection of artifacts or samples of students' work that provide a deeper, more thorough picture of a student's abilities. According to Valencia (1990), portfolios have four guiding principles. First, the artifacts should be authentic products of the ongoing curriculum and not pieces created only for evaluative purposes. Second, portfolios must be continuous and ongoing, assessing the process of learning rather than a single product. Third, portfolios must also be multidimensional, utilizing a wide range of potential indicators of attitudes, skills, and knowledge. Fourth, portfolios must allow for active collaboration between students and teachers so that assessment becomes a shared vision of what has been learned and where to go next. Materials in the portfolio may include such things as journals, checklists, writing samples, self-evaluations, learn-

ing logs, questionnaires, retellings, reading records, attitude measures, tests, audiotapes, videotapes, and photographs. Portfolios
encourage teachers to use a wide variety of indicators to evaluate
students and to keep a detailed record of achievements over time.

Portfolio assessment values the process of learning as well as the
product. It allows teachers and students to use assessment as an
integral part of instruction. This process-oriented, student-centered,
ongoing system fits well into multiage classrooms.

Teacher/Student/Parent Conference

One of the keys to multiage classrooms involves close communication between school and home. Every child needs to know that
both environments are supporting learning. Communication between home and school can take many forms: newsletters, personal
notes, telephone calls, home and school visits, and conferences.
According to Goodlad and Anderson (1987), "The parent-teacher
conference is the approach most universally advocated in the current
literature of reporting and is probably the most fruitful and effective
single means available" (p. 123). Conferencing should accommodate
the concerns of all the stakeholders. Conferences should be flexibly
scheduled and held whenever a need is perceived. These interactions
allow for the teacher, the student, and the parent to share successes
and concerns and to set goals for continual learning.

SUMMARY

Although each multiage classroom will look different from the
next, certain elements tend to be present in a majority of multiage
classrooms. Basic to a successful transformation of any classroom or
curriculum is an understanding of the philosophy and rationale
behind the configurations. It is essential for teachers and administrators to recognize early in the process of examining multiage grouping that no two classrooms will look the same—nor should they.

The curricular, instructional, and assessment pieces discussed in
this chapter support the philosophical perspective of multiage grouping. A prerequisite for teaching in a multiage setting is an under-

Common Beliefs

---

child-centered
activity-based
focus on process
hands-on learning
diversity is valued
students are self-regulating

Curricular and Instructional Elements

---

process writing
literature-based reading
thematic teaching
learning centers
math manipulatives
cooperative learning
peer tutoring
computer-assisted instruction
team teaching

Assessment Elements

---

ongoing, continuous
authentic
multidimensional
collaborative effort
informs instruction
use of portfolios

Figure 3.1. Common Elements Across Multiage Classrooms

standing of the elements of process writing, literature-based reading, learning centers, math manipulatives, cooperative learning, thematic teaching, peer tutoring, computer-assisted instruction, team teaching, and assessment strategies.

The time it may take for teachers and administrators to become familiar with the teaching strategies suggested in this chapter will be worth it in the long run. Success is assured by a well-prepared staff, not by a beautiful classroom environment or healthy financial support.

FOUR

What Can We
Learn From Practice?

Case Study: A Parent's Perspective

It's a typical evening at McDonalds and a group of parents are chatting while their children are playing in the play area.

"McMaster Elementary has been talking about multiage grouping for next year. Do you know anything about it?" asks Jane.

"Sarah is currently in a multiage classroom at her school," replies Kay. "She just loves it. She's in with a group of 6-, 7-, and 8-year-olds."

"But why would you put all those different ages of children together? What are the benefits?" questions Jane.

Tom, a parent of a "gifted" second-grade child overhears and says, "I certainly don't want Jennifer to be in a class with first graders. She'll never be challenged and I don't want her to simply 'teach' the first graders. How can the teachers possibly meet her needs?"

"I'm concerned about my son, Joey," adds Karen. "Joey has some very special learning needs and requires lots of individual attention. How can he ever keep up with the class, especially the second graders?"

"Well, I've found that Sarah is being challenged at her own level. It seems like there is plenty of opportunity for her to make choices about learning. She also loves being able to 'help' the other children when they need it or to be able to find a fellow student to help her if she needs it. It

seems that the students are much less dependent on the teacher for every-thing."

"I'd be interested in observing in some of these classrooms," says Jane. "I'd like to see what they really look like."

"Let's call and find a time to visit some of the rooms," suggests Kay.

"Great idea. I'm interested!" says Jane.

After reading reams of material about the philosophical base for multiage grouping, many teachers, administrators, and parents like the group at McDonalds still ask the question "What does it look like in practice?" This chapter contains the stories of four multiage settings, how they got there, and what they look like. The stories are all different, for each teacher and school is unique. Yet they share common attributes. They all focus on developmentally appropriate practices and utilize a variety of the common curricular and instructional elements that were discussed in Chapter 3. Each story is a success story. Though no one version is just the right one to duplicate for another site, the intent is to see how various schools successfully moved from traditional graded structures to multiage configurations.

The first school is Talahi Elementary. The multiage unit is part of a large school involving six teachers in three pairs, working with 6-, 7-, and 8-year-olds. Lincoln Elementary's multiage program is also an option within the school. Five teachers are currently involved, working with first, second, and third grade. The third model, Cambridge Elementary, runs a multiage program as a school within a school. There is a primary multiage group (P-MAG) encompassing first and second grade, and an intermediate multiage group (I-MAG) involving third and fourth graders. The last case study, Bethel, is a preschool with all 2½- to 5½-year-olds involved in a multiage setting.

Each school is still growing and changing, as all schools should. But here are their stories up to now.

Talahi

The Model

Talahi is a large elementary school with more than 930 students, spanning kindergarten through sixth grade. Although large, the school functions almost as a little city. The mission is to create a "sense of community" where every child feels safe. Talahi is located in St. Cloud, a city of 50,000 people, 60 miles west of Minneapolis. The students are predominantly white, although there is a higher representation of students of color in the school than is reflected in the city. Students represent a wide socioeconomic spectrum and come from a variety of family structures.

Discussions about multiage classrooms began before the school even opened its doors in 1990. The principal, a strong advocate of multiage grouping, led the teachers in exploring the concept. During the spring of the first year Talahi was open, the college of education at a nearby university offered a graduate class, focusing on developmentally appropriate practice and multiage grouping, to all faculty. During this class, faculty examined the traditional graded structure, discussed its strengths and weaknesses, and explored how developmentally appropriate practices suggested by NAEYC fit within the traditional structure. Grade level teams created a rationale and plans for organizing instruction. A group excursion to a multiage school in Wisconsin was undertaken as part of the course. As a result, teachers in the primary grades K-2 began to run "Wacky Wednesdays" during the 1991-1992 school year. On Wednesdays, children from kindergarten, first, and second grades were mixed, and lessons utilizing a variety of approaches were delivered for one half-day a week. The "Wacky Wednesdays" provided teachers with the experience of working with multiage groups.

The next year (1992-1993) brought a new principal and an informal utilization of multiage grouping. Teachers formed trios, with kindergarten, first-, and second-grade teachers involved. Some of these groups mixed a limited number of different age level students for reading and/or math instruction; other trios did not. About halfway through the school year, the teachers involved felt a need to explore the potential of a greater move toward multiage grouping. A series of four workshops was held, during which the teachers discussed the philosophy of multiage grouping and explored potential models for structure, curriculum, and instruction. As part of this in-service, teachers were asked to decide whether they were ready to move into the implementation of a multiage model. Six first- and second-grade teachers made a firm commitment to implement multiage grouping in the fall of 1993. The kindergarten teachers were also interested, but the half-day kindergarten configuration made it extremely difficult to work out an acceptable model for their inclusion. The other teachers involved in the in-service chose not to utilize a multiage structure. This decision allowed both a graded and a multiage model to be available so that parents could have a choice for their children.

The six teachers who committed to implement multiage grouping chose to create three teams, each consisting of two teachers. Each team was responsible for a first-grade section and a second-grade section, which they blended to create classrooms consisting of mixed grade levels. The three teams met on their own time in August to develop their structure and curriculum. Ultimately, each pair made decisions for its own team. Late in the summer, a new teacher hired by the school joined one of the teams to create a trio.

The decision to create multiage classrooms led to some physical changes in the classrooms. Doors were added to connect classrooms without having to utilize the hall, tables replaced desks, and classrooms acquired easels, blocks and other developmentally appropriate materials. The teachers made a commitment to sharing ideas and materials among the teams.

As school began in 1993, seven teachers and approximately 175 first- and second-grade students were involved in the multiage configuration. The rest of the school remained in separate grade level classrooms. Although the teachers involved in the project were comfortable with a multiage configuration for science, social studies, and health, they were much less comfortable with blending groups for reading and math. Therefore, during the designated math and reading instructional times, students were shifted back into age-segregated rooms, with a few exceptions. This gradual transition, utilizing a multiage structure for only part of the day rather than a headfirst dive, made the move toward multiage grouping much more comfortable for the majority of teachers involved.

A Typical Day

The 6-, 7-, and 8-year-olds enter the room together and make choices about what to do to begin the day. Stations are available for varied activities. This time allows the children to take on the responsibility for their own choices. Following the opening bell, the children come together for the 30-minute opening. During this time calendar, attendance, lunch count, and community building occur. Children are involved with patterning activities, number lines, reading, listening, and problem solving. Following the opening, the first graders move to one classroom and the second graders move to the other. Grade-level reading instruction takes place during the next hour. The students then go back to their multiage homeroom for a snack and recreation break. After the break, the students move into first- and second-grade groupings for an hour of math instruction, followed by lunch. During the afternoon, the students are back in their multiage configuration, where science, social studies, and health are taught. The teachers are following a 2-year cycle of topics of study in teaching science, social studies, and health concepts. Special classes, such as art, music, computers, and physical education, are built into different slots during the afternoon. Students stay in their multiage groupings for these classes. Each team of teachers has a common planning time to facilitate collaboration and communication.

What's Happening Now?

After the first year of multiage classrooms, the seven teachers involved in the multiage classrooms were satisfied with their year. They had positive feelings about the growth in their children, citing students' cooperation and nurturance as very positive outcomes. They also found their students were making more of their own decisions and taking on responsibility for their learning. The three teams started the 1994-1995 school year having developed a confidence in multiage grouping. The teachers' growing comfort level in working with a multiage model led to some changes in programming. Two of the three teams decided to keep multiage groupings all day Monday and Friday and to group by age for reading and math on Tuesday, Wednesday, and Thursday. The third team made continual modifications after losing one teacher due to budget cuts. The daily schedule for the new school year was similar to that of the year before.

7:30-8:00	Free Choice
8:00-8:30	Opening Activities
8:30-9:30	Reading*
9:30-10:00	Break
10:00-11:00	Math*
11:00-11:45	Lunch
11:45-2:10	Thematic units encompassing science, health, social studies Specials during this time (art, music, physical education)

Figure 4.1. Typical Daily Schedule for Talahi Elementary
*Students are homogeneously grouped for these activities.

Lincoln

The Model

Lincoln Elementary School, also located in St. Cloud, Minnesota, houses grades K-3. There are approximately 400 students and 15 classroom teachers. Lincoln has a high concentration of low socioeconomic class children, with 60% receiving free or reduced lunch. Students of color represent 10% of the population, with the largest representation from Southeast Asia. At least one third of the students qualify for special services under federally funded programs.

During the fall of 1990, the staff at Lincoln created a mission statement for their school that revolved around developmentally appropriate practices as outlined by NAEYC. In the spring of the next year, the principal of Lincoln realized he had a group of first-graders and a group of second-graders, neither group large enough for a separate teacher. The principal's commitment to developmentally appropriate practice, along with his own experience in a multi-age classroom, led him to ask one teacher if she might be interested in teaching the first- and second-graders as a multiage group rather than a split class. The teacher volunteered to take this mix of first- and second-grade students and create a multiage classroom. This teacher undertook a tremendous amount of reading on the subject, visited a multiage classroom, and spent the entire summer planning for her class. As the school year started, she adapted and changed her plans to meet the individual needs of the students. She had few age-appropriate materials available and used her imagination in creating appropriate hands-on, child-centered curricula. As the only multiage teacher among all traditionally age grouped classrooms, this teacher made all of her own curricular and instructional decisions.

The next spring, several Lincoln teachers who had observed the multiage classroom experience expressed interest in working in a multiage configuration. These teachers attended workshops, read materials, visited classrooms, and talked frequently with the first teacher. The following year, the multiage teacher moved up to remain with her students. A second teacher joined her in teaming with a second/third-grade combination, and the third teacher had a first/second-grade grouping.

During this second year, in-service was provided to the entire school regarding multiage grouping and meeting individual needs. A consultant also worked intensely with the small group of three multiage teachers over the course of the year. The three teachers continued to read and attend workshops dealing with multiage grouping. An informal network of teachers around the Central Minnesota area was established and met several times to discuss ideas and issues.

By the end of the second year, the three teachers had made a decision to blend grades 1, 2, and 3 for the following year. Two additional teachers formed multiage classrooms for 1994-1995 and all five of the teachers taught a 1-2-3 multiage classroom. Four of the teachers paired off into teams, and the fifth teacher decided to work alone with the support of the other four teachers.

A Typical Day

There are a number of similarities among the schedules of the five teachers. Both teams open the morning with a class meeting that covers calendar, singing, and sharing. They move into free time, where children are allowed to choose activities from among a number of stations. This is followed by "family" time where reading and

7:55-8:10	Handwriting*
8:10-8:35	Class Meeting
8:35-9:00	Explore time/free choice
9:00-9:15	Snack
9:15-10:30	Families (reading and language arts)
10:30-11:00	Centers (reinforcement in literacy)
11:00-11:40	Lunch
11:40-12:05	Read aloud to class
12:05-1:00	Flexible skills instruction in math*
1:00-2:00	Specials (Library, physical education, art, music)

Figure 4.2. Typical Daily Schedule for Lincoln Elementary
*Students are homogeneously grouped for these activities.

writing are addressed. There is "discovery" time, which encompasses science, social studies, and health. Students remain in their multiage configuration during all of these activities, along with art, music, physical education, and computers. For approximately 1 hour a day, the children are flexibly grouped for direct instruction in math and reading skills. Both teams utilize "book clubs," where children read from among five books of various levels. The books and discussion then focus on exploration of literary elements. In teaching reading, these teachers also use a substantial amount of poetry in addition to a wide variety of other genres.

The fifth teacher keeps all of her first-, second-, and third-grade students in their multiage configuration all day. She works with small, flexible groups within her individualized curriculum. Changes she has made in her schedule include the addition of a sharing time and one half-hour of free time for students every day.

Cambridge

The Model

Cambridge Elementary School, located in rural Cambridge, Minnesota, 30 miles north of Minneapolis/St. Paul, currently offers two separate and distinct learning environments for students. Parents may choose between conventional 1-year graded classrooms or 2-year multiage classroom units. The conventional classrooms service kindergarten through fourth-grade students. The two multiage units service primary (approximately ages 6-8) and intermediate (approximately ages 9-11) students.

As a school within a school, the Multi-Age Group (MAG) project is an attempt to establish a natural learning environment for children. Determined to develop a flexible, healthy, need-satisfying climate that benefits both students and teachers, the multiage units have been implemented as alternatives to conventional, graded classrooms. The multiage teachers at Cambridge Elementary have established that the MAG Unit has the following mission:

All students will achieve in an environment that promotes learning, appreciates differences, and builds self-esteem.

Beliefs:
- Recognizing that children progress developmentally, multiage grouping is appropriate.
- Recognizing that lifelong learning depends on acquiring an expanding variety of skills, "process learning" is emphasized.
- Recognizing that children learn in different ways, a variety of learning opportunities are provided that promote feelings of success.
- Recognizing that children learn in different ways, it is necessary to provide a variety of interactive learning opportunities that build self-esteem and self-worth.

Organization

In 1990 the Cambridge/Isanti School District faced budget constraints and possible staff reductions. With the full support of the building principal, three elementary teachers became interested in developing a cost-effective "family"-oriented program for third- and fourth-grade students. A literature search indicated a resurgence of interest nationwide in flexible grouping patterns that encouraged developmentally appropriate education in interactive and academically challenging environments.

Initially, the teachers met together and shared their personal philosophies of what education should be for children. Then wiping the slate clean, they began to discuss the potential for essential learning opportunities in a multiage setting. The district offered 2 paid summer work weeks to plan and organize the program. Knowing that 2 weeks would not be sufficient time to design a multiage unit, the teachers contributed the extra hours and days needed to be comfortable with opening the unit in the fall. The team visited other multiage school sites to see what was already operational and then proceeded to design their own hands-on curriculum package that emphasized process skills.

The first year of implementation included 120 third- and fourth-grade students, four full-time teachers, one part-time teacher, and one instructional assistant in two double rooms. Third-grade students and their parents were asked to make a 2-year commitment to the program, widening the parameter of time for teachers to introduce and integrate curriculum. The second year of implementation (1991) brought many changes. A Primary Multiage Group (P-MAG) was organized and developed for younger children in grades 1 and 2. Program and course competencies were written to help solidify the curriculum and provide direction for evaluating student performance.

Both MAG programs have grown to collectively include 300 students, 14 full-time teachers, several part-time teachers, instructional assistants, and support staff specialists who enrich and reinforce instruction. The teaching teams schedule regular planning times and often engage in team-building activities. Student daily schedules include both structured class time and time for choice in a self-directed learning center environment. Interdisciplinary curriculum connections incorporated into thematic units, with expectations appropriate for each child, create a more holistic approach to content and a learning environment that is rich in experience.

Socially and academically, students interact with students of different ages and developmental stages, much like a family, a workplace or any situation outside school. This collaborative expectation stimulates growth in the areas of promotive interaction, positive interdependence, and interpersonal group skills. Weekly student/teacher conferences, a checklist system, and portfolios help to

8:15-9:10	Homeroom
9:10-10:00	Specials (computers, physical education, music, art); Teacher Preparation Time
10:00-10:50	Math
10:50-11:50	Lunch
11:50-3:00	Thematic units

Students are heterogeneously mixed all day.

Figure 4.3. Typical Daily Schedule for Cambridge Elementary

evaluate student progress, encourage individual accountability, and provide regular responses to parents.

A Typical Day

Intermediate MAG students, organized into color groups, begin their day with a homeroom teacher. Routine tasks such as library book checkout, lunch count, attendance, and announcements are handled. Math, computers, art, music, and physical education instruction complete the 3-hour morning schedule. Following lunch and recess, the students have another 3-hour block of integrated thematic learning time, where they are grouped with other MAG students from different color groups. A rich blend of subjects including literature, social studies, science and health is taught, using cooperative skills that reinforce community, quality work, and life-long learning.

The Primary MAG is a very natural feeder program for the Intermediate MAG. Although Intermediate MAG students are never age-segregated, reading instruction issues compel the Primary MAG teachers to separate into "first" and "second" grade for part of each day, especially at the beginning of the school year. Primary students begin their day in an age-grouped classroom with a designated first- or second-grade teacher. The teachers team in pairs, a first-grade with a second-grade, and intentionally blend various ages and developmental stages as seems appropriate. The students are eventually integrated fully into thematic multiage experiences.

Bethel College Child Development Center

The Model

The Bethel College Child Development Center is situated on a college campus in metropolitan St. Paul, Minnesota, and serves children from the college community as well as the surrounding area. There are presently 66 children in attendance from diverse ethnic groups and socioeconomic classes, ages 2½ to 5½ years. The original intent behind the Child Development Center, when it opened in the fall of 1983, was to be a lab school and provide service to the college families. It continues to provide services by offering a 20% discount to college-affiliated families. A similar discount is provided to area low-income families. The Center employs four licensed teachers and student assistants and exists as a laboratory school for students in the college's early childhood program.

A Typical Day

During a typical day at the Center, the children spend most of their time in multiage groups, with age segregation for a short time each day when a small group might meet for a teacher-directed activity. The Center's physical layout is similar to a large home, with different rooms designated for different activities and interactions. The children know that only six students are allowed in a room simultaneously, and come and go without problems. Room designations do not vary; however, specific activities within the rooms change often. There is a dramatic play room, a wonder room, a block room, a large muscle room, a group time room, and an art room. On any day, a typical scene such as the following might ensue:

In "The Wonder Room," one of the many preschool resource rooms, some children ages 2½ to 5 years are involved in numerous activities. Having just observed the classroom snake consume his meal of a goldfish, and wondering about the relative size of each, Dan, a 5-year-old, asked Ryan, "Are you 5?"

Ryan: *"I'm 4, and he's 5."*
Tim: *"No, you're 5."*

Ryan: *"I'm 4!"*

Dan: *"Stand up straight. (The boys are back to back.) See, he's taller than me." (To Ryan) "Maybe you are 5."*

Tim: *"When I was little, I was almost to here (touches ankle).*

Dan: *"I'm the oldest. How old are you?" (To John, a 3-year-old) The boys move over to measure themselves against a shelf on the wall.*

John: *"I'm gonna be just like Teacher."*

Teacher: *"You'll probably be taller."*

John: *"Yeah, like a daddy."*

Several other children measure themselves for comparisons, first at the shelf, then looking through a magnifying glass, then nose-to-nose.

John: *"Hey, I'm bigger than you!"*

Ryan: *"Nahuh. Your hair's only up to here."*

This interaction is a learning experience that could not possibly have the same impact were it teacher-directed. The children enjoy each other, compare themselves with one another, and assist each other's cognitive development. In the dramatic play area, children can be heard expanding language by mimicking and trying out new roles and behaviors. In the block room an older child demonstrates both patience and self-esteem when a younger child knocks down his structure, apologizes, then watches it being rebuilt and says, "Hey, cool, how'd you do that?"

An example of a small group activity that is age-segregated and teacher-directed comes from an evaluation of a calendar by the "Bunny Group." The group decided that the pictures on the calendar did not represent people from ethnic groups other than European-American. Therefore, they decided to write a letter to the publisher of the calendar and dictated their thoughts to the teacher.

The teachers at Bethel have worked in a multiage setting for 4 to 10 years and feel very positive about its value for young children. They appreciate the homey, family-like setting; the way children act as role models for each other; their acceptance of differences, their sense of cooperation, and their opportunities to explore and develop interests and friendships.

SUMMARY

Beginning a new venture is always taking a risk: What needs to change? How can I be objective in examining my program, goals, and practices? How will my situation measure up with others? *What will the finished product look like?* The purpose of this chapter is to provide some glimpses of what multiage settings really look like in day-to-day practice. We certainly need to start a new venture with a set direction: goals, theories, and a research base. But we also want to know how rocky the path might be, when to expect roadblocks, and how to know when we have reached the journey's end.

A second goal of this chapter is to provide existing examples of multiage settings which all differ. Thus, you now have the same map with similar beginning and end points, but with numerous possible routes from one to the other. The models presented have originated differently, involve different age configurations, include individuals and teams of teachers, exist as complete settings or schools within schools, and segregate for various activities.

Learning from practice means taking what fits your particular situation, and avoiding pitfalls by recognizing others' pioneering mistakes. It involves visualizing students and staff within particular settings and comparing those with your personal vision, and then being creative and building your own model.

FIVE

How Do We Get Started?

Case Study: The Teacher's Perspective

A group of first-, second-, and third-grade teachers from McMaster Elementary are debriefing after visiting a multiage setting in a neighboring school district.

Ms. Johnson begins the discussion by saying, "I truly believe that multiage learning is appropriate for many children. But after what I've seen today, I am concerned about the labor-intensive environment for teachers."

Mr. Tiffen agrees, "Did you see all of the teacher-made materials in those classrooms? And the cupboards were full of supplemental literature books and math manipulatives! I'm not sure we've got enough materials to do the job in the way they are doing it."

"Well," says Mr. Gannon, "it's true we are going to have to be very creative with our budget next year. But though I'm convinced that we should try multiage grouping, I want to customize our program so that it really fits the needs of our students and their families. Although I liked many of the things I saw today, there were some ideas that I don't think are suitable for our situation. For one thing, I didn't much care for the schedule that was used to move children from class to class. It seemed quite rigid—too much clock-watching. I would hope that we can group more flexibly and not have to adhere to such a timetable every day."

Ms. Kemper's worried expression compelled the others to ask her to share her thoughts. "I am overwhelmed," she replied quietly. "I feel as if I'm in some very uncharted water here. Where do we begin? What steps do we take?"

Cleaning Closets

Ms. Kemper is right to wonder how to begin the transition process. Teachers and administrators must take definite steps, and sometimes these steps can seem overwhelming. The conventional system of graded classrooms is deeply entrenched and seems nearly impossible to change. One could compare the beginning of the transition loosely to cleaning a large house—one closet at a time.

Initially, when you open the front door, you see confusion and disarray. You recognize that it is time to do something about it, but haven't the immediate energy to tackle the entire job. So, in your mind, you schedule a day and time to clean *one* of the closets. When that day comes, you put on old, comfortable clothing and commence whatever self-talk it takes to get started. As you begin to pull everything out of the closet, you find yourself with a bigger mess than before. Things look worse and you begin to regret ever beginning the cleaning.

However, once it is all out in the open, you see what you have, begin to put things in order, discovering mislaid items and other things that are no longer useful. You clean methodically and with care. You are amazed at how involved the process is and feel a bit resentful of the time it has taken. Nevertheless, through hard work and perseverance, you eventually gain a neat, orderly closet; one that makes sense, meets the needs of your family, and can be opened when company comes.

Finally, as you gaze at the result, you resolve to never let your closet get so cluttered and disorganized again. Then, on to the next cleaning project. Sound familiar? Evolving from conventional classrooms to multiage units will necessitate some one-step-at-a-time closet cleaning.

There are essential steps to take in the process of transitioning from traditional to multiage classrooms. First, school staff must create a climate for conversation. Teachers and principals must change roles, with principals being willing and able to offer administrative support. Team building must be advocated and teachers should make plans for on-site visits to other multiage programs. Next, a program must be designed, with an understanding of "best" practices as an inherent principle. At all stages of planning and program development, parents must be encouraged to be involved.

Although the physical environment need not follow a specific plan, it is important to assess the type of room available. Finally, and of utmost importance, is the process of "letting go," during which teachers must begin relinquishing some of the control expected of them in traditional settings.

Create a Climate for Conversation

The first and most important step in transitioning to a multiage program is to create a climate within your school for genuine conversations about children and learning. Set aside blocks of time for teams of teachers to define, debate, determine, and develop the fundamental principles that drive a child-centered program. The movement for real change must come from teachers. They need to have the opportunity to voice their ideas and opinions in a safe, trusting environment, fearing no repercussions.

At times, there might be resistance to talking about educational issues. The tendency will be for teachers to discuss the *how to* when in fact it is critical that they first discuss the *why*. Not everyone is eager to participate in discussions that may show wide discrepancies in ideologies. Many prefer to go underground with their opinions as a way of avoiding conflict. They may talk regularly with colleagues who share similar convictions but rarely dialogue with those whose ideas are different. It must be understood, however, that conflict in and of itself is not bad. It can be the beginning of genuine, caring, and professional relationships, where the common goal of developing truly child-centered educational programs can be realized. It is healthy to dig deep, getting the issues on the table, thinking about our commitment to children.

Change the Roles of Teachers and Principals

As your school moves toward multiage grouping, the roles of staff need to change. Teachers should never act as primary sources of information. Imparting facts and knowledge, supported by an endless amount of task-oriented worksheets and activities, is not in the best interests of students entering the 21st century. Learning is social and demands that children of many ages and abilities come together to share and discover.

Teachers in multiage settings must be facilitators, helping children access information and acquire process and problem-solving skills. They must coach cooperative learning and prompt self-regulation habits. Teachers need to modify and coordinate curriculum to meet the students at their developmental levels, and continually inform parents and colleagues of progress. Most important, they have to engage their students in conversations about lifelong learning. It is their job to inspire and encourage children to be satisfied with nothing less than their best.

It naturally follows that the roles of principals need to change as well. In a healthy, conversational atmosphere, it is appropriate and necessary for the school principal to share personal hopes and dreams for the future. A visionary principal, who should also be a "master" teacher, ought to influence and motivate school faculty. When a principal becomes sidetracked by such routine administrative tasks as schedules, budget, and discipline, he or she has little credibility with teachers or parents regarding issues surrounding teaching and learning. These tasks would be better handled by a site-based management team or school council.

Enlist Administrative Support

Once teachers have established a common philosophy, it then becomes essential to enlist strong administrative support that will help promote program intentions. Although it is true that it is *not* effective for a principal to mandate philosophical changes, he or she should certainly encourage them. As teachers transition to multiage grouping, the principal can be of great help by supporting the innovations and buffering the impact of negative parents and staff. It is crucial to the well-being of teachers that they have regular support and encouragement from their principal.

Advocate Team Building

Advocate team building to create and support a spirit of renewal and growth, developing a healthy work organization where teachers sustain and encourage one another. True team building goes beyond the occasional social gathering and faculty meeting. Rather, it means intentionally setting aside time for teams of teachers to actively invest in one another, working toward developing trusting relationships. Real teaming takes place when *all* members of a team support each other in ways that establish a need-satisfying environment.

In his book, *The Quality School*, William Glasser (1990) discussed four needs basic to human nature: (a) the need to belong, (b) the need for power, (c) the need for freedom, and (d) the need for fun. When these needs are met within a teaming situation, everyone benefits, adults and children alike. The importance of spreading an umbrella of cooperation over the team cannot be overemphasized. Having teachers work together, get to know each other, cheer for shared successes, and develop collaborative skills is the critical foundation for true teaming.

Members of a team need to value diverse perspectives and believe in partnerships where all members have a voice. There should also be an awareness and acceptance of both strengths and weaknesses of individuals within the team, remembering that everyone makes contributions in unique and varied ways. Finally, it is essential for team members to candidly share their joys and disappointments with one another. Though perhaps awkward at first, genuine sharing is necessary to know what people are thinking and feeling in order to encourage, affirm, and problem solve together. Respectful listening and sharing are crucial. Establishing positive collegial relationships can diminish tension, self-doubt, and anxiety for teachers. Remember . . .

C — Celebrate the diversity of the team.

O — Offer ideas that improve instruction.

L — Learn from interaction with others.

L — Let bygones be bygones!

E — Everyone shares the success.

A — Allow for differences of opinion.

G — Give genuine support to others.

U — Use cooperative skills to team well.

E — Expect excellence from one another.

S — Share leadership responsibilities. (J. Anderson, 1993)

Encourage On-Site Visits

Visit several multiage school sites to gain a broader view of the possibilities. It is reassuring to actually see multiage classrooms in operation and find that teachers are enthusiastic about the program. Much time and talent have been expended on these program designs. Learn from what has already been done.

The Cambridge Elementary multiage programs have had countless teachers and principals come to see their classes in action. Reactions abound, ranging from total delight at the effortless way children of different ages learn together in such a natural environment, to disappointment that many elements of assessment have not yet been determined and/or implemented.

Recognize that someone else's innovations may not be suitable for your situation or should be modified to meet the needs of different student and teacher populations. It is tremendously helpful to schedule some dialogue time during your visits, to meet separately with the teachers implementing multiage programs. Their insights will benefit everyone involved. Be prepared to write down any questions you have before you go and jot down any ideas that occur as your observe.

Some schools are very generous about sharing their written materials. Others may not care to share—be sensitive. Expect to leave with images of what you do and do not want to include in your own program design. There will be times when your ideas are better: Trust your instincts.

The Program Design

Approach the program design slowly, giving enough time to plan, process, reflect, and inform. Clear the slate—put away the lesson plans and textbooks. Ask the critical question: What is essential learning for children? Trust your judgment as a professional educator. Look deep into the eyes of children and determine actual needs. Contemplate the possibilities. Think flexibly and boldly beyond state guidelines and curriculum committees.

Write everything down, beginning with your philosophy and beliefs. Be sure that your program is driven by clearly articulated outcomes/competencies. Once your true mission is established, then begin the arduous chore of designing assessments and tasks that will work toward your goals. For example, if one of your competency expectations is for students to demonstrate the ability to communicate orally, you must first determine the criteria for *how* they will show their learning. Perhaps you will ask students to discuss their learning progress at a parent/teacher/student conference, making sure that students understand the elements that go into conferencing. You will design tasks that relate to the process of getting ready for that conference, always keeping the original competency expectation—oral communication—in mind. The tasks themselves should never be assessed, as they are used solely for practice. The assessment is done during the final performance—the actual conference. Feedback is immediate and students are encouraged to self-evaluate as well. Every task should relate back to a predetermined assessment. Every assessment should relate back to a predetermined competency expectation.

Although it may seem overwhelming to plan and design in such a step-by-step manner, it will end the nightmare of requiring mindless busy work that is of no benefit to students. Your program will be defendable and credible. Realize that this process takes time—lots of time. You may or may not enjoy the luxury of having all of this in place before you begin your program. Regardless of whether you do, realize that this process is never done. It is ongoing and ever changing as the needs of children shift and vary. Reflect on what is being accomplished. Even if you feel confident that things are going well, evaluate and consider the results. Do they match your original goals and expectations?

As you begin to see results and acquire new knowledge of student progress, inform parents, colleagues, and administration. It is important to talk about the continuous learning of students in a multiage setting. There is a perception that because you have a wider range of ages and abilities, learning cannot take place. The opposite is true—learning happens *when* you have a wider range of ages and abilities, because there is a place for everyone. All students fit in and belong to a community of learners.

Learn About Best Practices

Moving toward multiage grouping necessitates the familiarization with best practices for teaching and learning. The curricular and instructional methods discussed in Chapter 3 are examples of current, research-based, appropriate practices. Reading the literature and research, attending workshops, and talking with other teachers about these practices are all important components in acquiring a knowledge base.

A quality program is determined by developmentally appropriate practice, as defined by the National Association for the Education of Young Children (Bredekamp, 1987). The essential philosophy of developmentally appropriate practices (DAP) is one that espouses child-initiated, child-directed, teacher-facilitated play and learning. Practices must be implemented according to their appropriateness for the interests, developmental levels, cultural backgrounds, and needs of the children in the group.

Developmentally appropriate practices assume that learning is accomplished best through an integrated curricular approach, which involves the whole child, that is, his or her social, cognitive, physical, and language developmental areas. Learning also takes place when it is relevant to children's experiences and is acquired in a concrete, real manner. Teachers guided by the philosophy of DAP act as facilitators of children's learning by providing a variety of activities, by challenging students, by adapting materials and being flexible in schedules, and by individualizing activities (Bredekamp, 1987).

The challenge to appropriately blend best practice ideologies is certainly before us. What makes this such an exciting profession to be a part of is the fact that we have the opportunity and responsibility to make good decisions about teaching and learning every day. The potential impact on our students is long-lasting. Continue to ask the critical questions, reflect on the *what* and *why* of teaching, and maintain an enthusiasm for children.

Involve Parents

Educate and inform parents about program design and goals before and during implementation. Include them in your process from the very beginning. Give them many opportunities to visit and volunteer: Conduct informational meetings regularly throughout the year, invite them to health fairs, maintain an open-door policy, utilize newsletters and conferences, and so on. Expect that any new program will be closely watched and judged critically. Give positive, sincere responses to questions and concerns, valuing diverse perspectives. Capitalize on the resources that parents bring into the classroom. Believe that parents are the experts when it comes to knowing their children's needs. Listen to their hopes and dreams and ask them to help you set personal learning goals for their children. Find and maintain a close link between home and school.

Look at Physical Environment

Considering a school's physical environment is one of the last steps in the process of transitioning from conventional classrooms to a multiage environment. Although the environment is important, it really has little to do with an ideology or belief system. Yet, many times logistics is an issue with teachers and/or administrators and can determine whether a program change is appropriate.

Multiage grouping can have many different physical arrangements. If you have an open environment (classrooms without walls or with movable partitions), you will be able to adjust and flexibly group students in small, medium, or large configurations. Open environments are conducive to learning stations, cooperative group projects, large class presentations, and special activities such as health fairs. The open atmosphere creates a spirit of invitation and extension: Learning is for everyone beyond traditional school walls. Students mix with a wider variety of children, and teachers are better able to team teach.

Closed classrooms, those that are built and equipped for 25 children and one teacher, can also be used for multiage grouping. Usually teachers in these settings either move from room to room with different mixes of students or have the same group of multiage students all day. Both are effective. It is more difficult to transform the single classroom into an experience rich, activity-oriented space, but it can be done. Rotating and sharing units, centers, literature, and manipulatives from class to class enlivens and broadens the possi-

- Create a Climate for Conversation
  - Set aside blocks of time for discussion of principles.

- Change Roles Along With the Rules
  - Be ready to facilitate rather than direct.

- Enlist Strong Administrative Support
  - Allow a visionary principal to inspire staff.

- Build a Supportive, Collaborative Team
  - Accept a variety of perspectives and voices.
  - Listen respectfully and share openly.

- Visit Other MAG Classrooms
  - Recognize the necessity for unique models.
  - Glean from those experienced in MAG practices.

- Design the Program With Deliberation
  - Start with a clean slate.
  - Allow time to plan, process, reflect, and inform.

- Become Familiar With Best Practices
  - Evaluate program goals and students' needs to mesh with practices.

- Involve Parents
  - Educate, inform, and invite parents.

- Look at the Physical Environment

- Let Go of the Need to Control
  - Practice flexibility and facilitation.
  - Enjoy the experience of watching students enthusiastically learn and develop.

Figure 5.1. Getting Started Steps

bilities for children. Changing teachers and flexibly mixing students help meet the learning needs as well.

Begin to Let Go

Letting go of control does not happen overnight. Teachers in multiage settings say that they release a little more control each year.

They begin to envision themselves as coaches or facilitators, rather than direct instructors. At the same time, teachers talk about how they develop a sixth sense with all that is occurring in their classrooms.

Dig deep; relinquish some of that control. Allow your wildest notions of what "might be" to happen. Maintain a generous spirit toward any skepticism from colleagues and parents as they look for significant differences. After all, you are challenging the traditional systems already in place in your school. Be open to student responses, both positive and negative. Give yourself permission to make mistakes and learn from them. Take joy as you begin to see a renewed enthusiasm for learning and participating in your classroom.

Yes, it takes hard work and perseverance. Yes, you will be overwhelmed and frustrated at times. But it is worth it. Your students are worth it. You will never go back.

SUMMARY

Similar to housecleaning, a move to multiage grouping can seem an overwhelming task. It is important to note that this change is not rapid. There are a number of important steps that will make the transition a little smoother. As the teachers at McMaster realize, multiage classrooms and models must be unique to each setting. They demand teachers' creativity and take a great deal of planning and rethinking of goals and program design.

SIX

What Do Teachers Have to Say?

Case Study: One Teacher's Perspective

The multiage teachers at McMaster Elementary have begun to reap the rewards of their endeavors and see the fulfillment of their goals as their students flourish within the classrooms. The traditional classroom teachers are not totally convinced that the multiage concept is really any different from their own approach to teaching. "I use process writing, whole language, and math manipulatives in my class," says Mr. Gannon. "I even try as often as possible to individualize instruction. What is the missing link here?"

Ms. Kemper smiled at the question. It was not a new one for her. "I understand that you utilize many of the same teaching strategies and that you individualize curricula. I know that you are as committed to your students as I am to mine. I appreciate the fact that you value what you were taught in your teacher-preparation programs and that you are hesitant to blow away with any seemingly new wind of reform. I also know that I cannot possibly explain to you what that 'missing link' is. It is as simple as a child's touch upon another's shoulder during a tutoring session, or as complex as designing a learning center for a diverse set of abilities. It is as mysterious as the art of teaching in any setting. Mr. Gannon, the missing link is not a curriculum, nor a strategy. It is not easily translatable. It must be experienced."

Planning and implementing change can be a very stressful and time-consuming process. As schools make the decision to move forward with multiage grouping, it is helpful to hear from others who have already made the journey. Through research, interviews, and actual classroom practice, the authors have gathered firsthand experience and information from practitioners. This should serve as a launching pad as you get under way with your work.

Teachers' Perceptions of Advantages of Multiage Grouping

View of Student Variables

In a recent study, teachers were asked about their perceptions of multiage grouping (Bacharach & Hasslen, 1994). The teachers discussed student variables such as problem-solving skills and self-esteem, and teacher variables such as opportunities for collaboration and enthusiasm for teaching. It was revealed that practitioners are overwhelmingly positive in their perceptions about student variables or characteristics associated with multiage classrooms. Prekindergarten and elementary teachers were most positive about students' sensitivity to others, ability to work with others, leadership qualities, problem-solving skills, involvement in child-directed activities, role-modeling and imitation, motivation to learn, verbal interaction, and vocabulary acquisition.

Teachers agree that multiage grouping is particularly conducive to students' growing awareness of others' viewpoints and behaviors as they work and learn together. Students develop leadership skills through their interaction with younger children. A 5-year-old demonstrates an exciting sense of empathy as she comforts a crying 3-year-old. Simultaneously, the younger child observes the caring behavior in the older child and begins to imitate it. All children are required to problem solve as they direct their own learning and find it necessary to refine and/or resolve interpersonal situations.

Students' self-esteem was rated as consistently positive by elementary teachers, who find that students demonstrate it in numerous ways. The teachers perceived higher self-esteem in students as they attain academic goals and acquire meaningful personal relationships. Self-esteem has been identified as an important effect of multiage settings, because students are not threatened by competition and are allowed to work at their own rate and within their interest areas and are not humiliated by being tracked. Ms. Kemper had been concerned about Tanya being tracked in a traditional classroom, where she would be compared with age mates rather than with her own rapid progress. Tanya had not only gained important cognitive skills, but had also blossomed socially as she proudly nurtured younger children in the class.

Altruistic behavior is another student variable rated favorably by teachers. Children in multiage classrooms find continuous opportunities to demonstrate prosocial behaviors as they interact with each other. Research is now revealing that even very young children are able to experience empathy. In multiage classrooms, younger children profit from older children who can be wonderful models of empathetic and caring behavior. Ms. Kemper found that her best classroom helpers were her students with special learning needs. These students, because they had experienced assistance from others, were very empathic, patient, and caring.

Critical thinking skills were identified by elementary teachers as positively associated with multiage groupings. Multiage classroom students, who are allowed more leeway to follow their own interests and delve deeply into topics, naturally analyze concepts and issues more thoroughly.

The overriding student variable, attitude toward school, is perceived positively across the board by all teachers in multiage settings. Students' excitement about learning grows out of their control over learning. They are provided the opportunities and flexibility to work alone or together, to explore and dig, to create and relate in the process of learning. Learning becomes fun, not work, as is often a distinction made by children in traditional classes, where work is separate from play or recess. Children in Ms. Kemper's room are given permission to participate in many different activities. The third-graders seem to particularly enjoy doing things traditionally reserved for first-grade students. Ms. Kemper smiles as her 8-year-olds "ride the horsey" down the hallways, delivering "mail" to other classrooms, or dress up with younger children in the dramatic play area. It is pleasurable to her when an older child continues to slip a hand into hers as they walk to the lunchroom.

View of Teacher Variables

The same study of teacher perceptions (Bacharach & Hasslen, 1994) found that teachers in multiage settings perceived as positive their relationships with parents, their individualized curricula, and their versatility in utilizing teaching strategies and activities. In addition to viewing these variables as positive, teachers discussed and affirmed the validation of their program goals through multiage grouping, their continuity of contact with the same students, their opportunities for collaboration with other teachers, individual time for students, and their overall enthusiasm for teaching.

As teachers responded to the benefits they derived from multi-age grouping, they pointed out that they could much more easily identify and work toward their programs' goals. This is in part because those goals were clearly identified and articulated to parents, staff, and administrators in the process of planning for multiage groupings. Teachers were guided by the basic goals inherent in developmentally appropriate practice that is child-directed, active, and individualized learning.

Teachers were especially appreciative of the opportunity to build rapport with students and their parents over the course of several years, as opposed to the shorter term and more sporadic relationships that may develop in traditional classroom groupings. Relationships with colleagues were also viewed as meaningful by multiage teachers who work in teams and collaborate on a daily basis. This also is in opposition to traditional schooling, which finds faculty often existing as islands within their individual classrooms. These opportunities for relationships, as well as the witnessing of students' excitement about learning, cause teachers to respond to multiage classrooms with an enthusiasm not always evident in traditional settings.

Teachers' knowledge of their students and their collaboration with other staff enable them to more naturally and readily individualize curricula. The goal of all education is to meet the needs of each individual and provide for the student's success. However, it is easy *not* to do that in a traditional setting in which students are grouped chronologically and taught from age/grade level material that assumes homogeneous abilities and interests. Multiage teachers are *forced* to teach individual children because of the classroom heterogeneity.

Advantages

- Improved social skills
- Modeling and peer imitation
- Development of leadership skills
- Focus on child-directed learning
- Lack of tracking
- Peer tutoring
- Greater comfort level
- Less competitive atmosphere
- Growing sense of responsibility of students
- Freedom for teachers in planning and teaching
- Working collaboratively

Disadvantages

- Developmental differences (esp. 3- to 5-year-olds)
- Schools within a school
- Antagonism from traditional classroom colleagues
- Too little training
- Inadequate time to plan
- Space—physical facilities
- Assessment

Figure 6.1. Advantages and Disadvantages of Multiage Grouping

Teachers' Perceptions of Disadvantages of Multiage Grouping

Teachers in the study (Bacharach & Hasslen, 1994) believed the greatest disadvantage of multiage groups in preschool settings to be the lack of sufficient numbers of staff. They also felt that there is such a wide developmental gap between 3-year-olds and 5-year-olds that it is difficult to group them together all the time. Some teachers were concerned, for example, that passive 3-year-olds might not receive the attention granted active 5-year-olds.

Elementary teachers responded to frustrations of being in schools within schools and facing antagonism from traditional classroom colleagues. They also felt that the lack of time for training and planning was a disadvantage. Often physical space became a problem for a multiage grouping's most effective operation.

Advice From Teachers

Many teachers would love the opportunity to sit down with a group of colleagues who have already made the move to multiage grouping. Although this type of meeting and conversation is highly recommended, it might not be an option for some teachers. To replace or supplement that conversation, we asked teachers what advice they would give to others venturing into multiage grouping.

1. You have to want to do it. Certainly, any situation's success calls for a positive attitude. However, teachers embarking on multiage grouping need to be excited enough about the concept and knowledgeable enough about its premises to overcome traditional barriers. It is simply not enough to have an administrator give the ultimatum to a staff.

2. You must be open-minded and flexible. The easy road to travel in life is the one with the ready-made road maps. No individual decisions are necessary. The map is plotted without our input and therefore without opportunity for any side trips or excursions that might be of particular interest to us. In multiage classes teachers must be continually flexible to deal with students' journeys, some of which are rapid and direct, others slow and distracted. Open-mindedness ensures that a teacher will not judge and try to redirect the student whose needs and interests are not the status quo.

3. You must believe in the concept of child-centered education, and your room must be child-driven. In order to provide evidence of success in a school system, it is necessary for teachers to guide students along a traditional curriculum and assess them according to standards for their age and grade. Teachers have schedules and curricula that they direct in order to meet their schools' goals and expectations. A child-centered concept is one that demands that teachers facilitate rather than direct the learning that goes on daily. Learning centers, whole language curricula, computer-assisted instruction, and peer tutoring are all ways that classrooms can be child-driven. Ms. Kemper is excited about the progress of her student, Tim, who has Attention Deficit Hyperactivity Disorder (ADHD). His mother is amazed that Tim, as a first-grader, has begun to perform double-digit mathematics. Tim directs his learning by working sometimes at a computer, sometimes with a friend, on his own time line with breaks when he needs them. He is not confined to a desk and a worksheet, both of which are inappropriate methods of learning for a child with ADHD.

4. *You have to be willing to let go of some control.* Teachers are expected to move their students along prescribed content areas and through specific skills during the course of a particular grade level. Allowing students to direct their own learning and work at their ability levels is difficult for teachers who are pressured by the expectations of the district or their peers. Letting go of individual control and allowing for student centeredness can also be a matter of pride for teachers who see themselves reflected in their students. Teachers describe this as one of the most difficult changes to undertake, yet one of the most critical for the multiage program's success.

5. *You must throw aside your fears and be willing to take risks.* What will parents think if their children are not reading the traditionally prescribed textbooks? How will colleagues react to a noisy class in which students are talking excitedly about their projects? What if there are few recognizable success stories by the end of the first year of a multiage group? Moving away from traditional to multiage groupings flies in the face of all that we are used to. Change is risky, and teachers stepping into a multiage setting must be strong enough and sufficiently prepared to meet challenges that are ahead.

6. *Visit other multiage classrooms: You get to see not only what you want to do, but also what you don't want to do.* The model for your multiage classroom will be custom-designed for your students and your situation. Visiting other multiage classrooms will provide you with some encouragement, some examples of classroom happenings, and certainly some ideas. However, no classroom is perfect, and rather

than setting yourself up for disappointment, go on a visit with an openness about possibilities and not probabilities.

7. Find a support network: the principal, other teachers in your building or the area, parents, a Teachers Applying Whole Language (TAWL) group, and so on. It is difficult enough to undertake a move away from any norm, but it can be an especially lonely enterprise for a teacher beginning the journey to transform a classroom setting. A support group is essential for more than moral support. Like-minded professionals can assist in the articulation of program goals, in the sharing of ideas for individualizing curricula, and in the creation of new and varied teaching strategies. Ms. Kemper and her area-wide multiage teaching colleagues formed a support network. The teachers look forward with enthusiasm to the network's quarterly meetings. Parents who are enthusiastic about multiage groups act as avenues for communication and provide marvelous PR to other parents and community members.

8. Make sure your entire school understands what you are doing. Sometimes those of us in education are the field's most resolute skeptics. It feels as though every few years we are enveloped in some new "reform" and are expected to adapt to its edicts with wholehearted enthusiasm. In the case of multiage grouping, it is rare that an entire school system will be asked to adhere to its pattern. However, it *is* essential that the school staff understand the concept and its rationale. Multiage teachers must keep the channels of communication as well as the doors to their classrooms open. This prevents widespread myths and interfaculty bickering.

9. Build respect for each other's choices of structure. Part of educating others about any concept, and specifically that of multiage grouping, is also accepting others' perspectives and preferences as valid and worthy. There is no one right way in education, and it is much more pleasant and productive to work within your choice of structure knowing you have the respect of colleagues.

10. Parental involvement is crucial: You must communicate well and involve the parents as much as possible. The involvement of parents is essential at all levels of their students' education. Parental involvement is a crucial aspect of multiage classes because it is an absolute necessity for parents to understand and support the concept. The actual involvement of parents in the classroom will assist their understanding of the rationale for multiage settings and their enthusiasm for children's self-directed and enthusiastic learning. In Ms. Kemper's room, parents become actively involved by reading with students, providing learning centers, leading small groups, and so on.

11. Make sure you have lots of planning time before you move into the implementation stage. Remember the amount of planning that went into your preparation for your first teaching position? Every activity was thoroughly defined and designed. Every minute of the day was scheduled, and every eventuality and its consequence contemplated. Despite the number of years you may have taught, you must allot the same amount of time now, not so much for *pre*planning as *re*planning. In place of a prescribed lesson plan, textbook, and worksheet, how will you provide learning opportunities? Without proper planning, multiage groups can be disastrous.

12. It helps to have at least one other adult (an aide or parent volunteer) for assistance. Many teachers in multiage classes find that an additional adult in the room is most welcome. This person can be useful as a facilitator of student/student interactions, as a provider of materials for an inquiring student, as a listener, a reader, or a game player. In other words, this adult will not serve the purpose of the traditional aide, who corrects worksheets or wipes tables, but will be involved in interactions with the students.

13. Have a school leader who helps facilitate communication and answers questions about the process. It is comfortable in a storm to have an anchor. Similarly, it is helpful during the planning and implementation phases of multiage grouping to have an individual designated to serve as the spokesperson for the concept and process. This will alleviate the spread of myths and misconceptions. However, this does not relieve the need for all faculty to be informed and articulate about the principles underlying multiage grouping.

14. Make sure you have a strong foundation in literature-based reading, math manipulatives, process writing, and other holistic practices. Although no one practice is unique to multiage classrooms, such holistic practices as these are essential components for working with children in individualized, developmentally appropriate ways. It is essential that teachers understand these practices, feel comfortable with them, and utilize them enthusiastically.

In all of these holistic practices, children support and assist in each other in learning. In Ms. Kemper's class one day, 8-year-old Lisa was overheard in a conversation with 6-year-old Marvin. "What do you want to be when you grow up ?" she asked. "A king," Marvin responded proudly. "Oh, that's very good," Lisa smiled. "I'll write that down and you can copy mine." As a newer student watched this scenario unfold, she ran to Ms. Kemper and reported that Lisa and Marvin were cheating. To this accusation, Lisa responded, "This is not cheating. Ms. K. says its a compliment when someone else looks at your paper."

15. Be prepared to devote a lot of time to your multiage classroom, especially in the first year or two. In order to ensure success in the early years of a multiage classroom, a teacher may need to expend more time and energy planning, executing, and assessing learning. Don't expect to feel totally comfortable your first year. Ms. Kemper spent months involved in study and curriculum evaluation prior to beginning with multiage grouping. As she began the first year, she found herself devoting time to networking, to reworking curricula, to creating learning centers, and to restructuring schedules and groupings.

16. Move into the changes at a speed that is comfortable for you. Any time we feel rushed, we also tend to feel anxious and ill-prepared for the task at hand. You may find that at the outset you are more comfortable with a partial multiage scheduling situation. As has been said many times, it is essential that your multiage program be streamlined for your particular setting. If you are a deliberate person who needs to have things well in hand before moving ahead, you must determine the amount of time you need to prepare for a multiage classroom. Your state of mind and enthusiasm or discomfort will affect your students.

17. Allow yourself time to grow. Be patient with yourself and the children. Have you ever been given a plant about which you know little, if anything? In your attempt to assist its growth, you may provide it with too little sunlight or too much water. Moving into a MAG setting is a similar process of growing and learning together for both teachers and students. You all need to get used to each other and become knowledgeable about what it takes for healthy and successful growth.

Issues in Multiage Grouping

Moving into the 21st century with the study of multiage grouping, we recognize a number of issues that call for continued research and examination. Documentation of case studies, along with empirical research methods, will help to address these issues. Some issues and questions identified by practitioners include:

1. What impact does multiage grouping have on students with identified special needs?
2. How can we best train our faculties to utilize multiage grouping?
3. What physical structure limitations exist and how can we remove them?
4. How can we best inform all the players (parents, administrators, students, other teachers)?
5. Are there materials that are not age/grade level bound?
6. How do we deal with the issue of a school within a school when only some of the rooms are multiage?
7. Is there a need to have small group experiences that are not multiaged? If so, for what subjects, and how often?

Many schools have already dealt with these issues effectively, and others are presently experimenting with solutions. Their stories need to be told.

SUMMARY

Teaching in a multiage classroom is perceived as a positive endeavor by teachers. Their students are perceived to be interacting in ways that enhance self-esteem, develop leadership skills, enable peer tutoring, provide opportunities for modeling and imitation, enhance verbal skills and vocabulary acquisition, promote altruistic behavior, allow for problem solving and critical thinking, and improve attitudes toward school.

Teachers view their roles more positively as they value ongoing contact with the same students and their parents, collaborate with other teachers, individualize their curricula, and utilize diverse strategies and activities.

Frustrations are perceived as growing out of limitations set by school district expectations for student outcomes, parental expectations and lack of understanding, textbook and material inappropriateness, lack of planning time, traditional teacher antagonism, and lack of space.

Multiage grouping is not a panacea. It will not create good teachers or schools out of poor ones. It will not automatically create a better learning environment or greater opportunity for students. As with any innovation, the individual teacher is the key to success. It takes a knowledgeable, caring, and committed teacher to successfully implement multiage grouping. We sincerely hope that this book provides important information for teachers ready to take the journey from traditional graded classrooms into the exciting world of multiage grouping.

References

American Association of School Administrators (AASA). (1992). *The nongraded primary*. Arlington, VA: Author.

Anderson, J. (1993). *Collegial support*. Unpublished paper, St. Cloud State University, St. Cloud, MN.

Anderson, R. (1993). Return of the nongraded classroom. *Principal, 77*(3), 9-12.

Azmitia, M. (1988). Peer interaction and problem solving: When are two heads better than one? *Child Development, 59*, 87-96.

Bacharach, N., & Hasslen, R. (1994, March). *Classroom teachers' perceptions of the social effects of multiage groupings in early education*. Paper presented at the annual conference of the Association of Childhood Education International, New Orleans.

Bandura, A. (1977). *Social learning theory*. Englewood Cliffs, NJ: Prentice Hall.

Bredekamp, S. (Ed.). (1987). *Developmentally appropriate practice in early childhood programs serving children from birth through age 8*. Washington, DC: National Association for the Education of Young Children.

Broadby, F. (1982). *Permanent part-time employment: A preliminary investigation* (Study No. 72). Tasmania: Education Department Research Branch.

Bronfenbrenner, U. (1989). Ecological systems theory. In R. Vasta (Ed.), *Annals of child development* (Vol. 6, pp 187-249). Greenwich, CT: JAI Press.

Brown, A. L., & Palincsar, A. (1986). *Guided cooperative learning and individual knowledge acquisition* (Technical Report No. 372). Champaign, IL: Center for the Study of Reading.

Bruner, J. S. (1960). *The process of education.* Cambridge, MA: Harvard University Press.

Buckholdt, D. R., & Wodarski, J. S. (1978). The effects of different reinforcement systems on cooperative behaviors exhibited by children in classroom contexts. *Journal of Research and Development in Education, 12*(1), 50-68.

Calkins, L. (1988). *The art of teaching writing.* Portsmouth, NH: Heinemann.

Cambridge Elementary MAG Program. (1991). Unpublished document. Cambridge Elementary School MAG Committee, Cambridge, MN.

Carbone, R. F. (1961/62). A comparison of graded and non-graded elementary schools. *Elementary School Journal, 62,* 82-88.

Cushman, K. (1990). The whys and hows of the multi-age primary classroom. *American Educator 14*(2), 28-32, 39.

Department of Elementary-Kindergarten-Nursery Education. (1968). *Multi-age grouping: Enriching the learning environment.* Washington, DC: National Education Association.

Erikson, E. (1950). *Childhood and society.* New York: Norton.

Farr, R. (1992). Putting it all together: Solving the reading assessment puzzle. *The Reading Teacher, 46,* 26-37.

Freedman, P. (1981). *A comparison of multi-age and homogeneous age grouping in early childhood centers.* Urbana, IL: ERIC Clearinghouse on Elementary and Early Childhood Education. (ERIC Document Reproduction Service No. ED 207 673)

French, D. C. (1984). Children's knowledge of the social functions of younger, older, and same-age peers. *Child Development, 55,* 1429-1433.

French, D. C., Waas, G. A., Stright, A. L., & Baker, J. A. (1986). Leadership asymmetries in mixed-age children's groups. *Child Development, 57,* 1277-1283.

Furman, W., Rahe, D. F., & Hartup, W. W. (1979). Rehabilitation of socially withdrawn preschool children through mixed-age and same age socialization. *Child Development, 50,* 915-922.

Gaustad, J. (1992). *Making the transition from graded to nongraded primary education.* Eugene, OR: Oregon School Study Council. (ERIC Document Reproduction Service No. ED 343 282)

Gelman, R., & Baillargeon, R. (1983). A review of some Piagetian concepts. In P. H. Mussen (Ed.), *Handbook of child psychology: Vol. 3. Cognitive development* (4th ed., pp. 167-230). New York: John Wiley.

Glasser, W. (1990). *The quality school.* New York: HarperCollins.

Goldman, J. (1981). Social participation of preschool children in same versus mixed-age groups. *Child Development, 52,* 644-650.

Goodlad, J. I., & Anderson, R. H. (1963). *The nongraded elementary school* (rev. ed.). New York: Harcourt, Brace & World.

Goodlad, J. I., & Anderson, R. H. (1987). *The nongraded elementary school.* New York: Teachers College Press.

Graves, D. (1983). *Writing: Teachers and children at work.* Portsmouth, NH: Heinemann.

Graziano, W., French, D., Brownell, C. A., & Hartup, W. W. (1976). Peer interaction in same- and mixed-age triads in relation to chronological age and incentive condition. *Child Development, 47,* 707-714.

Hammack, B. G. (1975). Self-concept: Evaluation of preschool children in single and multiage classroom settings. *Dissertation Abstracts International, 35,* 6572-6573.

Hartup, W. W. (1979). The social worlds of childhood. *American Psychologist, 34,* 944-950.

Howes, C., & Farver, S. A. (1987). Social pretend play in two year olds: Effects of age of partner. *Early Childhood Research Quarterly, 2,* 305-314.

Johnson, D., & Johnson, R. (1987). *Learning together and alone* (2nd ed.). Englewood Cliffs, NJ: Prentice Hall.

Katz, L. G., & Chard, S. C. (1989). Engaging children's minds. Norwood, NJ: Ablex.

Katz, L. G., Evangelou, D., & Hartman, J. (1990). *The case for mixed-age grouping in early education.* Washington, DC: NAEYC.

Kim, S. H. (1990). *The effect of cross age interaction on socially at risk children.* Unpublished doctoral dissertation, University of Illinois, Urbana.

Kohn, A. (1992). *No contest: The case against competition.* Boston: Houghton Mifflin.

Lougee, M. D., & Graziano, W. G. (1986). *Children's relationships with non-age peers.* Unpublished manuscript.

Lougee, M. D., Grueneich, R., & Hartup, W. W. (1977). Social interaction in same- and mixed-age dyads of preschool children. *Child Development, 48,* 1353-1361.

Mann, H. (1970). Seventh report to the Massachusetts Board of Education, 1843. In E. P. Cubberley (Ed.), *Readings in public education in the United States* (pp. 287-288). Westport, CT: Greenwood.

Mobley, C. (1976). *A comparison of the effects of multi-age grouping vs. homogeneous age grouping in primary school classes of reading and mathematics achievement.* Unpublished doctoral dissertation, Nova University.

Mounts, N. S., & Roopnarine, J. L. (1987). Social-cognitive play patterns in same-age and mixed-age preschool classrooms. *American Educational Research Journal, 24*(3), 463-476.

Muse, I., Smith, R., & Barker, B. (1987). *The one-teacher school in the 1980's.* Las Cruces, NM: ERIC Clearinghouse on Rural Education and Small Schools. (ERIC Document Reproduction Service No. ED 287 646).

Piaget, J. (1973). *The psychology of intelligence.* Totowa, NJ: Littlefield & Adams.

Pratt, D. (1983, April 11-15). *Age segregation in schools.* Paper presented at the annual meeting of AERA, Montreal.

Reuter, J., & Yunik, G. (1973). Social interaction in nursery schools. *Developmental Psychology, 9,* 319-325.

Roopnarine, J. (1987). The social individual model: Mixed-age socialization. In J. L. Roopnarine & J. E. Johnson (Eds.), *Approaches to early childhood education* (pp. 143-162). Columbus, OH: Charles E. Merrill.

Shatz, M., & Gelman, R. (1973). The development of communication skills: Modification in the speech of young children as a function of listener. *Monographs of the Society for Research in Child Development, 38* (5, Serial No. 152).

Shepard, L. A., & Smith, M. L. (1990). Synthesis of research on grade retention. *Educational Leadership, 47*(8), 84-88.

Slavin, R. E. (1987). Ability grouping and student achievement in elementary schools: A best-evidence synthesis. *Review of Educational Research, 60,* 293-336.

Slavin, R. E. (1990). *Cooperative learning: Theory research and practice.* Englewood Cliffs, NJ: Prentice Hall.

Stright, A. L., & French, D. C. (1988). Leadership in mixed-age children's groups. *International Journal of Behavioral Development, 11,* 507-515.

Thompson, G. (1991). *Teaching through themes.* New York: Scholastic.

Topping, K. (1988). *The peer tutoring handbook: Promoting cooperative learning*. Cambridge, MA: Brookline.

Valencia, S. (1990). A porfolio approach to classroom reading assessment: The whys, whats and hows. *The Reading Teacher, 43,* 338-340.

Vygotsky, L. S. (1978). *Mind in society.* Cambridge, MA: Harvard University Press.

Wakefield, A. P. (1979). Multi-age grouping in day care. *Children Today, 8*(3), 26-28.

Way, J. W. (1981). Achievement and self-concept in multiage classrooms. *Educational Research Quarterly, 6*(2), 69-75.

Whiting, B. B. (1983). The genesis of prosocial behavior. In D. Bridgeman (Ed.), *The nature of prosocial development* (pp. 221-242). New York: Academic Press.

Whiting, B. B., & Edwards, C. (1988). *Children of different worlds: The formation of social behavior.* Cambridge, MA: Harvard University Press.

Wiseman, D. (1992). *Learning to read with literature.* Boston: Allyn & Bacon.

Suggestions for Further Reading

Anderson, R., & Pavan, B. N. (1993). *Nongradedness: Helping it to happen*. Lancaster, PA: Technomic.

Chase, P., & Doan, J. (1994). *Full circle: A new look at multiage education*. Portsmouth, NH: Heinemann.

Goodlad, J., & Anderson, R. (1987). *The nongraded elementary school*. New York: Harcourt Brace.

Kasten, W., & Clarke, B. (1993). *The multi-age classroom: A family of learners*. Katonah, NY: Richard C. Owens.

Katz, L. C., Evangelou, D., & Hartman, J. (1990). *The case for mixed-age grouping in early education*. Washington, DC: NAEYC.

Glossary

Cognitive theory: a theory supporting the idea that learning is a dynamic process with individuals as active constructors of their own development.

Computer-assisted instruction: the use of computers and software to teach, practice, or apply concepts.

Cooperative learning: a collection of strategies designed to have students work in groups to foster interdependence and cooperation among learners.

Developmentally appropriate practice: curriculum and instructional strategies that are individualized and child-centered.

Ecological theory: a theory supporting the idea that development is a result of the interrelationships of an individual with the family, community, society, and world.

Heterogeneous grouping: the random grouping of students so that groups represent a variety of abilities, gender, race, and socioeconomic levels.

Homogeneous grouping: the grouping of students who are similar in some trait, usually ability, to decrease differences among the group.

Learning centers: areas in the classroom where collections of materials and activities from concrete to abstract are available for students to learn, reinforce, or apply concepts.

Literature-based reading: an instructional reading approach that uses children's literature to teach reading.

Math manipulatives: the use of concrete materials and activities that allow students to physically manipulate items to understand a mathematical concept.

Multiage grouping: the purposeful placement of students more than 1 year apart in the same classroom.

Peer tutoring: students assisting other students to grasp a concept.

Portfolio: a collection of artifacts documenting a student's progress over time.

Process writing: an approach to teaching writing that focuses on learning and valuing the processes that are a part of writing instead of focusing solely on the product.

Psychosocial theory: a theory supporting the idea that success or failure of individuals dealing with a series of psychological and social challenges is determined by the individual's relationships and by demands placed on the individual by society.

Social learning theory: a theory supporting the idea that development is the product of observation, imitation, and identification with others.

Sociocultural theory: similar to the social learning theory, this theory stresses the importance of understanding the expectations, tools, skills, and interactions provided by a child's culture.

Spiral curriculum: a curriculum that builds on earlier concepts and enables students to acquire and manipulate new information as well as to advance beyond the present dealings with information.

Team teaching: the simultaneous collaboration of two or more teachers for an entire educational program for a group of students.

Thematic teaching: the use of a central theme around which all subjects are taught.

Index

CORWIN
PRESS

The Corwin Press Logo—a raven striding across an open book—represents the happy union of courage and learning. We are a professional-level publisher of books and journals for K-12 educators, and we are committed to creating and providing resources that embody these qualities. Corwin's motto is "Success for All Learners."

DATE